HARVARD STUDIES IN ENGLISH
VOLUME XV

THE LIFE AND DEATH OF
WILLIAM MOUNTFORT

BY

ALBERT S. BORGMAN

LONDON : HUMPHREY MILFORD

OXFORD UNIVERSITY PRESS

THE LIFE AND DEATH OF WILLIAM MOUNTFORT

BY

ALBERT S. BORGMAN

CAMBRIDGE
HARVARD UNIVERSITY PRESS
1935

PREFACE

I WISH to thank the officials of the British Museum, the Bodleian Library, the Public Record Office, the Harvard College Library, and the Boston Public Library for many courtesies; the authorities of the British Museum and the Henry E. Huntington Library and Art Gallery for permission to reproduce as illustrations materials from their collections; and the rectors of St. Clement Danes, St. Giles in the Fields, and St. Martin's in the Fields, Middlesex, for permission to examine the parish registers. I wish also to thank for many gracious acts of assistance Professor Leslie Hotson, Miss Addie F. Rowe, Mrs. Frances B. Griffin, and my colleagues, Professors B. Sprague Allen, Theodore F. Jones, and Winthrop R. Ranney. My greatest debt of gratitude is due to Professor Hyder Rollins for invaluable suggestions and innumerable kindnesses.

One must proceed with caution when treating the theatrical history of the late seventeenth century. The qualifying phrase — "Judging from the incomplete records" — is to be understood with every generalization. When years are mentioned, they are given in the New Style. On page 124 and following, where conversation reported at the trial of Lord Mohun is quoted, the spelling "Mountford" is changed to "Mountfort."

A. S. B.

BROWN HOUSE,
NEW YORK UNIVERSITY,
January 2, 1935.

CONTENTS

LIST OF ILLUSTRATIONS

THE LIFE AND DEATH OF
WILLIAM MOUNTFORT

INTRODUCTION

SOME of the most fascinating pages in *An Apology for the Life of Colley Cibber*, a book which, despite Fielding's satire, will always prove a delight to lovers of the theatre, characterize the principal players at Drury Lane in 1690. From a vantage-point of nearly fifty years, the aging actor and dramatist looks back at the days when, as a stage-struck lad of nineteen, he commenced his career. And so enthusiastically does Cibber describe the giants of the theatre of his youth that the reader for a moment willingly forgets the age of Ibsen and Shaw and wishes he could attend a performance given by Their Majesties Servants at the Theatre Royal, with Betterton and Mrs. Barry playing the leading rôles, with Leigh and Nokes sustaining the comic scenes, and with the lovely Anne Bracegirdle appealing in epilogue for a full house on the third day.

But the art of the actor is of all arts the most transitory, and Cibber properly laments that "the animated Graces of the Player can live no longer than the instant Breath and Motion that presents them, or at best can but faintly glimmer through the Memory or imperfect Attestation of a few surviving Spectators." His attestations, imperfect as Cibber says they are, do, in his fourth and fifth chapters, succeed in bringing vividly to the interested reader the peculiar abilities of thirteen actors and actresses of two centuries and a half ago. Not the least important in this group was William Mountfort, a player of versatility who was rapidly growing in his art, and who might have received the mantle of Betterton had he not been killed in a fit of jealous anger by Captain Richard Hill.

The description which Cibber has given of this young actor — who was not more than ten years his senior, and who was able to portray equally well the rake and the fop, the lover in tragedy and the fine gentleman in comedy — invites the antiquarian of the theatre to further inquiry. The following study of the life and death of William Mountfort may be considered as an extended footnote to the *Apology*. The author realizes that it is impossible to say anything about Mountfort's histrionic powers in addition to what has been written by Cibber, but he does hope, with the aid of musty quartos and yellowing documents, to trace the brief career of this actor and author and to present him in his relations with his contemporaries of the days when Dryden, Shadwell, and Southerne were writing for the theatre and when Congreve was preparing for his brief but memorable flight.

PART I

LIFE

PART I

Life

I

ON DECEMBER 1, 1682, King Charles, Queen Catherine, and the maids of honor attended a performance at the Theatre Royal in Drury Lane. The occasion was important, for the play, *The Duke of Guise* by Dryden and Lee, was the first new work to be presented by the United Company. The manuscript had been ready several months before, but because of complaints made to the lord chamberlain that the principal character was intended to represent the Duke of Monmouth, the acting had been prohibited on July 18. Dryden then waited upon his lordship and desired him to compare the tragedy with its historical source. Nothing happened until the expiration of several weeks, when the play was returned to the co-author without any indication whether or not it might be acted. Then it was insinuated that the king himself was represented as Henri III; but Charles did not allow these allegations to convince him that the play should be permanently prohibited, and on October 29 he signified his pleasure that it might be presented.[1]

1. Dryden, *The Vindication of The Duke of Guise*; *The London Mercury*, No. 34 (July 28–August 1, 1682); P.R.O. L.C. 5/16, p. 101, L.C. 5/145, p. 120 (Nicoll, pp. 10, 311); L.C. 5/144, p. 291. In Allardyce Nicoll, *A History of Restoration Drama* (Cambridge, 1923), are listed many of the entries in the lord

The Duke of Guise was produced at a time when the war between the conflicting political parties was being fought in the theatre as well as in parliament. Practically every dramatist of note had his say, either in play proper, prologue, or epilogue, about Whigs and Tories, the Popish Plot, and the Exclusion Bill. Naturally Dryden, as laureate and therefore as a loyal adherent of the king, was violent in his opposition to the Whigs and had recently taken time to pillory in masterly fashion Shadwell and Settle, the principal dramatists of that much-hated faction. The Whigs were, of course, prompt to find fault with anything that the leading writer of the Tory party had to offer; and on the very evening when the king and queen were present at the theatre, they did not forbear indicating their displeasure. Their pamphleteers were also ready to point out the resemblances between the play and the contemporary situation: in the assembly of the States-General at Blois they found a parallel to the parliament held at Oxford in March, 1681, and in the murder of the Duke of Guise they were willing to detect an encouragement to assassinate their idol, the Duke of Monmouth.

But in that audience of December 1, 1682, there must have been many seasoned theatregoers whose interest lay not in what political hangers-on saw fit to applaud or hiss but in the play itself and the actors who appeared in it. Such persons would, of course, remember that in the early part of this very year there had been two theatrical com-

---

chamberlain's warrant books which are of interest to students of late seventeenth-century drama. In every instance where I draw materials from these documents already recorded by Professor Nicoll, I indicate the fact. When his name does not appear, it is to be understood either that he does not list the entry or that his quotation from or summary of the material omits some words or ideas of which I make use.

panies in London — the King's, acting at the house in which they were now gathered, and the Duke's, performing at the theatre in Dorset Garden; that the King's Company, because of gross mismanagement, had ceased to act in April; that the remnants of the King's Company had then joined forces with the Duke's Company; and that, two weeks before, on November 16, the United Company had made its first appearance at Drury Lane. These theatregoers would also observe that the parts in *The Duke of Guise* were largely taken by former members of the Dorset Garden group.

Chief among these was Thomas Betterton, who appeared as the ill-fated Guise. For several years principal player in the Duke's Company, he now became the undisputed leader of the English stage. His associate as director of acting, William Smith, who had often played rôles of nearly the same importance as those assumed by Betterton, was cast for the blunt and honest Colonel Grillon. The part of the latter's niece, Marmoutier, the beloved of the Duke, was played by Mrs. Elizabeth Barry. This triad of Betterton, Smith, and Barry had on countless occasions acknowledged applause at Dorset Garden, recently as Lear, Edgar, and Cordelia in Tate's happily ending perversion of Shakespeare, as Jaffier, Pierre, and Belvidera in Otway's tragedy, and as Piercy, Henry VIII, and Anna Bullen in Banks' pathetic *Vertue Betray'd*. The other woman's part, that of the Queen Mother, was essayed by Lady Slingsby, who, before Mrs. Barry came into prominence, had divided the honors of being leading actress at the Duke's Theatre with Mrs. Betterton.

The only former member of the rival company to have an important part on this occasion was Edward Kynaston,

who was fittingly cast as the King. An actor of female
rôles at the time women were first introduced to the London stage, he had, in the days when the King's Company
was at its best, played third to Hart and Mohun: for instance, he was Harcourt to Hart's Horner and Mohun's
Pinchwife, Morat to Hart's Aurengzebe and Mohun's
Emperor, and Cassio to Hart's Othello and Mohun's Iago.
None of his earlier associates who had distinguished themselves as actors — William Cartwright, Philip Griffin,
Cardell Goodman, or Joseph Haynes — played in *The
Duke of Guise*, although in the future they were all to
appear with the United Company.

Any one of the first three persons just mentioned or
Joseph Williams, who had frequently supported Betterton
in such parts as Polydore in *The Orphan* or Edmund in
King Lear, would probably have been a better choice than
Thomas Percival for Malicorne, the conjurer who has
made a compact with the Prince of Hell. The scene in
which he appears with the evil spirit Melanax, played by
Thomas Gillo, although in Dryden's opinion one of the
best in the tragedy, was murdered in the acting. Among
the colleagues of Percival and Gillo to attain positions of
greater distinction in theatrical history than either of
them, but in *The Duke of Guise* cast for insignificant rôles,
were Samuel Sandford and John Bowman. The former,
whom Cibber terms the "*Spagnolet* of the Theatre," was
because of his "low and crooked Person" eminently fitted
to play the villain; the latter, singer as well as actor, had
during the previous five years appeared in a varied repertoire of characters, and was to live on as "the last of the
Bettertonian school" until well past the first quarter of the
next century.

Unlike Dryden's earlier play, *The Spanish Friar*, the present offering did not make use of the abilities of any of the four excellent comedians, all of whom had formerly belonged to the Duke's Company. There were no parts suited to James Nokes or Anthony Leigh; and Cave Underhill and Thomas Jevon had to be contented with the unimportant and non-humorous bits of the Curate of St. Eustace and the Duke of Mayenne. The inimitable Nokes, whose first entrance in a play was invariably a signal for laughter, and the mercurial Leigh were an unsurpassable pair, and many an author wrote with an eye to their special talents. Thus Shadwell was assured of a good third day when Nokes was the boisterous Sir Samuel Hearty and Leigh the precise Sir Formal Trifle in *The Virtuoso*, and Otway could not complain when they acted Sir Davy Dunce and Sir Jolly Jumble in *The Soldier's Fortune*. Nokes also played Polonius to Betterton's Hamlet; and Leigh, in a period when political questions were of greatest concern, could equally well personate Tegue O'Divelly, the Irish priest, in *The Lancashire Witches*, an anti-Tory play, and Antonio, a caricature of the leader of the Whigs, in *Venice Preserved*. Underhill, who was called by Cibber "a correct and natural Comedian," and whose Gravedigger in *Hamlet* became famous, was particularly admired for his presentations of heavy and stupid characters. The first to play Palmer in Etherege's initial effort, he outlived his three fellow-comedians and was able to create Sir Wilful Witwoud in Congreve's last comedy. The youngest of the group, Jevon, who was then in his thirtieth year, satisfied his audiences in both dancing and acting, and for that reason he was later to be in demand as Harlequin.

The Duke of Guise treated the women comedians no better than the men, and so Mrs. Katherine Corey and Mrs. Ellenor Leigh were without parts. Mrs. Corey, who had been a member of the King's Company from the days when women first began to act in London, and who was the only one of that early band of seven to appear with the United Company, had identified herself with a wide array of characters. She it was whom Pepys called Dol Common because of her superlatively fine acting in Jonson's comedy. She was also well-known to the theatregoer as Mrs. Otter in *The Silent Woman*, Abigail in *The Scornful Lady*, and Widow Blackacre in *The Plain Dealer*; and she showed her versatility by being the original Octavia in *All for Love*. Mrs. Leigh, on the other hand, had acted with the Dorset Garden troupe at various times during the previous dozen years, the most important of her efforts probably being Lady Woodvil in *The Man of Mode*. Her specialty — that of elderly women on the trail of young lovers — was to reach its climax in Lady Wishfort.

This far from Homeric catalogue of the most important members of the United Company, both those who acted in *The Duke of Guise* and those who were without parts in that tragedy, would not be complete without mention of two of the younger players, Susanna Percival and William Mountfort, both of whom will figure largely in the following pages. Mrs. Percival, formerly of the King's Company, had before the union been Winifred, the Welsh jilt, in D'Urfey's *Sir Barnaby Whigg*. Mountfort, from Dorset Garden, had but little to do as Alphonso Corso in the play by Dryden and Lee; and it is doubtful whether the theatregoers of 1682 would have been able to prophesy that in the ten years of life he had before him he would be

able to attain a position among the actors second only to
that occupied by Betterton.

Mountfort, who at the time of the union had, in the
words of the prompter John Downes, grown to the matu-
rity of a good actor, was eighteen years of age or there-
about.[1] Nothing is known of the early part of his life
other than what the "Account" prefixed to the 1720 edition of his plays tells us. He was "the Son of Captain
Mountfort, a Gentleman of a good Family in *Staffordshire*," [2] and he "spent the greatest Part of his Younger
Years in that County, without being bred up to any Em-
ployment." Since "his Gaiety of Temper and Airy Disposition . . . could not be easily restrain'd to the solitary
Amusements of a Rural Life," he betook himself to the
city and became associated with the Duke of York's players at the Dorset Garden Theatre. His name — "Young
Mumford" — first appears opposite the part of the boy at
the inn in *The Counterfeits*, a play attributed to John Lean-
erd and produced as early as May 25, 1678.[3] Two years
after speaking the four lines allotted to him in this comedy,
he had a more fruitful opportunity as Jack, the awkward

1. His age is given as twenty-two on the day of his marriage, July 2, 1686.
See footnote 1 on p. 24. In a deposition dated October 22, 1691, he is said to be
"about 27 yeares" of age. A photostat of this document, P.R.O. C. 24. 1141/11,
is among the materials collected by Professor Leslie Hotson for use in *The Commonwealth and Restoration Stage*, preserved in the Theatre Collection of the
Harvard College Library.

2. Although the name "Mountfort" or "Mountford" appears often in
books dealing with Staffordshire, I have been unable to identify the Captain
Mountfort in question. It is possible that he may have been either Simon
Mountfort or Edward Mountfort, the sons of Sir Edward Mountfort of Bescote;
or Thomas Mountfort or Simon Mountfort, the sons of Will. Mountfort of Wal-
sall. See *Staffordshire Pedigrees Based on the Visitation of that County made by
William Dugdale Esquire Norroy King of Arms in the Years 1663–1664*, p. 173
(Publications of the Harleian Society, LXIII).

3. Nicoll, p. 311.

barber's man who is forever interlarding his remarks with "Forsooth," in *The Revenge; or A Match in Newgate*, an adaptation of Marston's *The Dutch Courtesan*. Although on the stage only in the second act, he had two good brief scenes with Jevon, who played the gamester Trickwell and as such borrowed Jack's barber's implements, and Leigh, who was Dashit, the gullible vintner, cheated by means of Trickwell's cleverness. These two are the only parts that we may say with certainty were played by Mountfort before November, 1682; but in the four years preceding the performance of *The Duke of Guise* he had undoubtedly trod the boards in many an insignificant rôle.

Of less individuality than Jack in *The Revenge* was Mountfort's part in *The Duke of Guise*. The friend of the king, Alphonso Corso, was made to serve largely as a "feeder" of lines to Kynaston's Henri III and Smith's Grillon. He was, however, given momentary surcease from being a mere tool of exposition when, in the council scene in the third act, he was allowed to make the bloody suggestion that Guise be immediately put to death:

> I would advise you, Sir, to call him in,
> And kill him instantly upon the Spot.

II

For some time after the uniting of the two companies, the actors were more willing to revive old plays from their combined stores than to venture something entirely new, and so, says George Powell, "*the Poets lay dorment; and a new Play cou'd hardly get admittance, amongst the more precious pieces of Antiquity, that then waited to walk the*

Stage." [1] The actors' preference is easily understandable,
for in the earlier days plays belonging to one company
could not be presented by the other, and doubtless Betterton had often cast an envious eye towards Hart, who had
a monopoly on Brutus and Othello. From contemporary
quartos we know a few of the parts that Mountfort played
in these revivals. When *Julius Caesar* was given with
Betterton as Brutus, Smith as Cassius, and Kynaston as
Antony, he was Metellus Cimber, the conspirator who
presents the petition in the senate-chamber. Possibly a
more satisfying rôle from the point of view of the actor,
although in a less important play, was that of Mr. Nonsense in *The Northern Lass*. This awkward Cornishman
with his continual use of "I protest and vow" offered food
for laughter in the scene where he proves an unwelcome
suitor and in the passage where he repeats his instructions
in parrot-fashion.

Although no comment has been preserved concerning
Mountfort's acting of Mr. Nonsense, there are frequent
references to his appearance in another of Brome's comedies. In *The Jovial Crew* he doubled Master Talboy and
the Lawyer. Talboy is also a rejected lover, but when he
is crossed he resorts to tears. The fact that Amie, the
justice's niece, prefers her uncle's clerk to him, is reason
enough for a series of showers. Cibber was to remember
him in this part and to write "in his Youth he had acted
Low Humour with great Success, even down to *Tallboy*"; [2]
and Oldys, or whoever wrote *The History of the English
Stage* that Curll printed, was to record "the first particular
Notice taken of him on the Stage was in Acting the Part of

1. *The Treacherous Brothers* (London, 1690), "The Preface to the Reader."
2. *Apology*, ed. R. W. Lowe (London, 1889), I, 211.

Tall-Boy." [1] Mountfort himself did not forget the lachrymose lover when, in the prologue to his first play, he tells the audience that even if they damn his tragedy,

True Talboy *to the last I'll Cry and Write.*

Near the time when he was appearing in these revivals, Mountfort acted in one of the few new plays, *Dame Dobson*, a comedy which the author, Edward Ravenscroft, thus designates in the prologue:

No Line in this will tempt your minds to Evil,
It's true, 'tis dull, but then 'tis very civil.

It seems to have been a failure,[2] despite the fact that the action frequently tended toward the farcical. It contains one long part, that of the "cunning woman" named in the title and played by Mrs. Corey. Although an adaptation from the French, *Dame Dobson* suggests the technique employed by Ben Jonson. Like Dol Common, Mrs. Corey's most famous rôle, the dame makes capital out of the gullibility of mankind. Having the reputation for helping people out of difficulties, she is eagerly visited by all sorts of persons: the goldsmith's son, who desires an enchanted sword; the skeptical gentleman, who is convinced of her powers when he learns where his lost pistols are; the indiscreet lady, who is helped to a husband. Mountfort was not required in this instance again to impersonate an awkward suitor; instead he was Mr. Hartwell, a young man of sense distracted by jealousy. In order to try the effect of absence upon Lady Rich, he spends a month at Tunbridge

1. *The History of the English Stage, from the Restauration to the Present Time . . . By Mr. Thomas Betterton,* "London: Printed for E. Curll, at Popes-Head in Rose-Street, Covent Garden, MDCCXLI," p. 32.
2. Gerard Langbaine, *An Account of the English Dramatick Poets* (Oxford, 1691), p. 419.

and has the report brought back to London that he has
found another sweetheart. Lady Rich, in her turn, becomes
jealous and goes to the supposedly omniscient woman for
information. Hartwell, having wind of her plans, returns
to the city, and with the assistance of some tricks contrived by the good dame he convinces her of his love.

It appears, from a manuscript list,[1] that Mountfort also
had a part in *Valentinian*, the Earl of Rochester's alteration of Beaumont and Fletcher's tragedy, which was acted
at court on February 11, 1684, and which proved a profit-
able venture for the company. In the rôle of the "sweet-
fac'd" eunuch Lycias, it was his lot to carry the lying
message to Lucina, played by Mrs. Barry, and to converse
with her in heroic couplets, and, in the last act, after being
discovered with the lustful emperor, to receive his death-
blow at the hands of the general Æcius, acted by Betterton.

It is possible that Mountfort appeared in *The Silent
Woman* on January 15, 1685, on one of the last occasions
that King Charles visited the theatre. Verses by Matthew
Prior — to be quoted later — inform us that the young
actor had "play'd so well . . . *Jack Daw*." [2] This pretender to learning, who scribbles madrigals and considers
that he utters as good things every hour as are to be found
in Plutarch and Seneca, has many opportunities to draw
laughter from the audience, especially in the scene where
he is made afraid of the cowardly Sir Amorous LaFoole.
His predecessor in the rôle, when Jonson's comedy was
given by the King's Company, was Robert Shatterel. Un-

---

1. The cast as printed by Downes is incomplete. Mr. Montague Summers
in a note on this play in his edition of *Roscius Anglicanus*, p. 237, gives the names
of the other actors, including Mountfort, and their parts from "a MS. list"; but
he neglects to indicate where the list may be found.

2. See p. 22.

fortunately no casts of the revivals of the play by the
United Company have been preserved; but it is not unlikely that Kynaston and Mrs. Corey retained their old
parts of Sir Dauphine and Mrs. Otter on the occasions that
Mountfort acted Sir John Daw.

With the exception of the foolish knight in *The Silent
Woman*, the rôles which have been mentioned so far as
played by Mountfort have in the main been slight, the
best of them offering an opportunity for some eccentric
characterization. We now come to what may be considered his first full-length part, Sir Courtly Nice. The subject of the comedy in which this character appears had
been suggested to John Crowne by King Charles, and the
faithful dramatist had set to work with the hope of preferment. But he was doomed to disappointment. On the
last day of rehearsal, early in February, 1685, as he was
approaching the theatre, he was surprized to find Cave
Underhill leaving the building. From him he learned of
the king's fatal illness. Of course, all plans for the opening
performance had to be postponed. But when the period
of mourning was over, *Sir Courtly Nice* was the first new
play to be produced.[1]

There was no question of its success. The author wrote
triumphantly, "This Comedy has rais'd it self such a fortune in the World, I believe it will not soon run away."
The actors were fully equal to the several capital parts
which Crowne had provided. Kynaston sustained the
longest rôle, the over-zealous Lord Belguard, who puts
numerous spies upon his sister for fear she may be con-

---

1. John Dennis, *Original Letters, Familiar, Moral and Critical* (London,
1721), I, 51–54; Arthur F. White, *John Crowne His Life and Dramatic Works*
(Cleveland, 1922), pp. 137–145.

taminated, but who is finally convinced that such a proceeding is futile and that virtue is a woman's only guard. Leigh appeared as the clever Crack, who for a consideration dresses as an East Indian merchant and pretends so to abhor women that he falls into agonies in their presence. Underhill and Gillo were the ardent Tory Hothead and the hypocritical Presbyterian Testimony, ever violently quarreling.

The author reserved his best strokes of characterization for Sir Courtly, the second of the three great fops that late seventeenth-century playwrights have given to the literature of the theatre. The first, Sir Fopling Flutter, acted by Smith, made his bow to the audiences at Dorset Garden in March, 1676. Although Smith's name appears in casts of plays produced by the United Company until 1687, he apparently did not choose to create Sir Fopling's successor, and thus caused fortune to knock at the gate of a younger man.

In common with all fops, Sir Courtly gives great thought to his dress; but he is also, to use the author's quaint phrase, "overcurious in his Diet." He is particular that no hands shall touch his food. He sends his butler to bring salt from his country-house forty miles away, because London salt is "pawm'd by Butlers and Waiters." He cannot endure wine since he traveled in France and saw the natives press grapes with their naked feet. This nicety appears also when he tells how his linen is made in Holland by women who dip their fingers in rose water. Going to comedies is his aversion, because they are "so ill-bred and sawcy with Quality" and the theatre is filled with his "odious Sex — that have not always the most inviting smell," but at tragedies it is different, for then "the House is all lin'd with Beauty." He avows that if a lady is to fasten upon his heart, "it must be with her Teeth." Feeling that "Men of Quality are above Wit," he does not write plays, but he occasionally composes a prologue or a song, one of which he sings to Leonora. He finds eternal happiness in contemplating his charms in a looking-glass. And it is the looking-glass which eventually leads to his confusion. While he is admiring himself, Leonora slips out of the room and her amorous Aunt enters. He makes love, and then turns around to discover what has happened. There is a scene of cross-purposes: he is asking for consent to wed Leonora, and the Aunt thinks that she herself is the person meant. Finally, resort is made to the stage-worn device of having Sir Courtly wed a lady in a vizard. When she unmasks, the beau discovers that he has been duped into marrying the Aunt; and, vowing revenge, he takes his leave amid general laughter.

Mountfort's acting of the fop was praised on every hand. The author of the "Account" mentions that Mountfort "gain'd a great and deserved Reputation, as a Player; particularly in Acting the part of Sir *Courtly Nice*." Matthew Prior, in one of his satires, refers to Mountfort, "That play'd so well Sir *Courtly*." [1] The actor's skill was also remembered in "*The Lover's Session. In Imitation of Sir* John Suckling'*s Session of Poets*":

> *Montrath* was in Foppery conceiv'd another
> Of *Whitehall* true Breed, Sir *Nices* Twin Brother;
> None could tell, so alike all their Follies did seem,
> Whether he acted *Mumford*, or *Mumford* him. [2]

---

1. See p. 22.
2. *Poems on Affairs of State*, II (1703), 162.

But Cibber, who was to join the company a few years after the first performances of this play, and who, some years after Mountfort's death, was to succeed to this rôle, has these words to say — generous words when one considers that they come from the originator of the third of the fops, Sir Novelty Fashion:

[He] could at once throw off the Man of Sense for the brisk, vain, rude, and lively Coxcomb, the false, flashy Pretender to Wit, and the Dupe of his own Sufficiency: Of this he gave a delightful Instance in the Character of *Sparkish* in *Wycherly's Country Wife*. In that of Sir *Courtly Nice* his Excellence was still greater: There his whole Man, Voice, Mien, and Gesture was no longer *Monfort*, but another Person. There, the insipid, soft Civility, the elegant and formal Mien, the drawling Delicacy of Voice, the stately Flatness of his Address, and the empty Eminence of his Attitudes were so nicely observ'd and guarded by him, that he had not been an entire Master of Nature had he not kept his Judgment, as it were, a Centinel upon himself, not to admit the least Likeness of what he us'd to be to enter into any Part of his Performance, he could not possibly have so completely finish'd it. If, some Years after the Death of *Monfort*, I myself had any Success in either of these Characters, I must pay the Debt I owe to his Memory, in confessing the Advantages I receiv'd from the just Idea and strong Impression he had given me from his acting them. Had he been remember'd when I first attempted them my Defects would have been more easily discover'd, and consequently my favourable Reception in them must have been very much and justly abated. If it could be remembred how much he had the Advantage of me in Voice and Person, I could not here be suspected of an affected Modesty or of over-valuing his Excellence: For he sung a clear Counter-tenour, and had a melodious, warbling Throat, which could not but set off the last Scene of Sir *Courtly* with an uncommon Happiness; which I, alas! could only struggle thro' with the faint Excuses and real Confidence of a fine Singer under the Imperfection of a feign'd and screaming Trebble, which at best could only shew you what I would have done had Nature been more favourable to me.

During his first appearances in the part, Mountfort was fortunate in having the character who is a complete antithesis to Sir Courtly, the "morose, ill natur'd, negligent Fellow" Surly, played by Griffin, who Downes avers so excelled in the rôle that "*none succeeding in . . .* [it] *. . . have Equall'd him.*" Since Surly sleeps in his hat and talks to his love Violante as he would to a hector who has stolen his money, he proves an admirable foil to Sir Courtly. While in his cups, he treats the fop rudely and insults him, after being challenged to a duel, by naming a squirt as his weapon. The two women appearing in scenes with Mountfort were Mrs. Barry, who played Leonora, a part which Cibber thought to be of little value, and Mrs. Leigh, whose especial forte of personating "modest stale Maids that had miss'd their Market," made her well-fitted to be the amorous and envious Aunt.[1]

By his acting of Sir Courtly in May, 1685,[2] — two and a half years after the performance of *The Duke of Guise*, — Mountfort had shown the frequenters of the London playhouse that he could meet the older and more experienced members of the company on their own level and that, with proper opportunities and encouragement, he ought to go far in his profession.

1. *Apology*, I, 163, 307.
2. King James, his queen, and the maids of honor attended performances at the theatre on May 11, 1685, and May 10, 1686. It was acted at Whitehall on November 9, 1685, and November 3, 1686. L.C. 5/147, pp. 68, 125, 260 (Nicoll, pp. 312–313).

III

In the month following the first performances of *Sir Courtly Nice*, London was startled by the news that the Duke of Monmouth had landed at Lyme with the hope of overthrowing King James and of establishing himself upon the English throne. The energies of the patrons of the theatre were turned from such unimportant matters as Dryden's elaborately staged opera of *Albion and Albanius* to the more serious question of defense. But the quixotic attempt ended in disaster, and five weeks after his landing "King" Monmouth paid the extreme penalty on Tower Hill. His death did not end all thoughts of the rebellion, for early in September Judge George Jeffreys, of odious memory, started on his western circuit. The chief justice's cruelty — doubly cruel because accompanied by a savage sort of wit — has become proverbial. His boast that he had hanged more traitors than all his predecessors since the Conquest was rewarded by his royal master, who had him appointed to the office of lord chancellor.

His evenings were frequently devoted to revelry, and the story has come down that on one occasion he and the Lord Treasurer Rochester became so intoxicated that they stripped themselves to their shirts and would have climbed a sign-post to drink the king's health if they had not been prevented.[1] Apparently he had no lack of convivial companions or persons who were ready to cater to his amusement. Among these was Mountfort. A glimpse at one of Jeffrey's entertainments in which the actor fig-

---

1. *The Memoirs of Sir John Reresby of Thrybergh, Bart. . . . Written by Himself. Edited from the Original Manuscript by James J. Cartwright* (London, 1875), p. 357.

ured has been preserved by Sir John Reresby, who dined with the lord chancellor on January 18, 1686:

> After dinner the Chancellor, having drunk smartly at table (which was his custom) called for one Montfort, a gentleman of his that had been a comedian, an excellent mimic, and to divert the company, as he called it, made him give us a cause, that is, plead before him in a feigned action, where he acted all the principal lawyers of the age, in their tone of voice, and action or gesture of body; and thus ridiculed not only the lawyers, but the law itself. This, I confess, was very diverting, but not so prudent as I thought for so eminent a man in so great a station of the law; since nothing could get a man more enemies than to deride those whom they ought most to support.[1]

Whatever the passage may reveal concerning the taste of the lord chancellor, it is an interesting commentary on the ability of Mountfort. It also indicates that the actor may have temporarily withdrawn from the company. Mountfort's popularity with Jeffreys is furthermore attested by Matthew Prior, when in his "Satire upon the Poets, in Imitation of the Seventh Satire of Juvenal" he shows how in two instances players have been more fortunate than poets and suggests that a person desiring preferment would do well to attend John Sheffield, Earl of Mulgrave, who as lord chamberlain was brought into frequent association with the actors:

> Were *Shakespear*'s self to live again, he'd ne'er
> Deg'nerate to a Poet from a Player.
> Now *Carlisle* in the new-rais'd Troop we see,
> And chattering *Mountfort* in the Chancery;
> *Mountfort* how fit for Politicks and Law,
> That play'd so well Sir *Courtly* and *Jack Daw*.

---

1. *Idem*, p. 355.

Dance then attendance in slow *Mulgrave's* Hall,
Read Maps, or court the Sconces till he call;
One Actor's Commendation shall do more
Than Patron now, or Merit heretofore.[1]

The meager available dramatic records make no reference to Mountfort during the year 1686,[2] and it may be that he remained for some time in the household of the chancellor. Possibly he had been willing to withdraw from the company because of ill-treatment by Betterton. A statement in the reply of the patentees to the petition of the players, dated December 10, 1694, mentions the fact that Betterton had been allowed to "brow beate and discountenance young Actors as Mr Giloe Carlisle Mountfort & others & keeping in Impropper persons in parts & turning out putting in & advancing whom he pleased." [3] The joining of Mountfort's name with that of Carlisle,[4] who appears not to have acted after 1685, and with that of Gillo, who died in the latter part of May, 1687,[5] probably places these unfortunate experiences during the first five years following the union of the companies. After that time Mountfort had little reason to complain of the parts that fell to his share.

1. Matthew Prior, *Dialogues of the Dead, and other Works in Prose and Verse*, ed. A. R. Waller (Cambridge, 1907), pp. 56–57.

2. It should be noted that royalty attended performances of *Sir Courtly Nice* on May 10 and November 3, 1686 (Nicoll, p. 313).   3. L.C. 7/3.

4. Also spelled "Carlile." He was probably the James Carlisle who was commissioned ensign in the Duke of Norfolk's regiment of foot on June 20, 1685, ensign in the Earl of Lichfield's regiment of foot on July 15, 1686, and lieutenant in the same on April 1, 1688. At the Revolution, the colonel, lieutenant-colonel, major, and four senior captains of this regiment adhered to James II. On December 31, 1688, Henry Wharton became colonel. Carlisle was captain when the regiment was reviewed at Dundalk camp in October, 1689. He was killed at Limerick. See Charles Dalton, *English Army Lists and Commission Registers*, I, 167, II, 33, 81, 157, III, 109, 403.

5. Thomas Gillo was buried at St. Bride's on May 31, 1687.

In the year when theatrical records are silent concerning Mountfort, church records reveal the important fact that the most promising of the younger actors was married to the most promising of the younger actresses. In the register of St. Giles in the Fields, Middlesex, appears the entry that "William Munford of St. Martins in y̆ Fields Middlesex & Susanna Percivall of this Parish Midd:sex were married July 2ḍ 1686 by licence." [1]

Mrs. Mountfort, then aged nineteen, had before her marriage played several secondary rôles, such as Mrs. Susan, the awkward country girl, and Mrs. Jenkin, the Welsh woman, in *Dame Dobson*, the jilt Constance Holdup in *The Northern Lass*, Rachel in *The Jovial Crew*, the slighted mistress Juliana in *The Disappointment*, and Prudentia in Tate's *A Duke and no Duke*. Probably the best liked of her early parts was that in Jevon's popular farce of Nell, the cobbler Jobson's wife, which was said by D'Urfey, in disgust at the failure of *The Banditti*, to be "*now a much better Character then* Sempronia [in *Catiline*] *or* Abigail [in *The Scornful Lady*]." [2]

Husband and wife acted together in two plays in 1687, *The Island Princess* and *The Emperor of the Moon*. The first, a poor revision of Fletcher by Nahum Tate,[3] was given in April with Smith and Mrs. Cook in the leading

1. Copied from the register. In *Allegations for Marriage Licences issued by the Bishop of London, 1611 to 1828*, II, 307 (Publications of the Harleian Society, XXVI), is this entry under date of July 2, 1686: "William Mountfort, of S⁺ Martin's in Fields, Bachʳ, 22, & Mʳˢ Susanna Peircivall, of S⁺ Giles in Fields, Spʳ, 19; consent of parents; at S⁺ Giles in Fields."

2. Thomas D'Urfey, *The Banditti* (London, 1686), Epistle Dedicatory "To . . . Sir Critick-Cat-call."

3. Arthur C. Sprague, *Beaumont and Fletcher on the Restoration Stage* (Cambridge, Massachusetts, 1926), p. 139, asserts that the alteration is based upon the stage-version of 1669, and not directly upon the Fletcher text.

rôles of Armusia and Quisara. The lines of Piniero, as his name appears in the original play, or Pymero, as he is called in this version, have been so cut and garbled that to take the part must have been a rather thankless task for Mountfort. Perhaps his best scene was the short passage in the fifth act with Panura, the princess' woman, played by his wife, where she offers to conduct him through the vault, but is apprehensive lest he mistreat her. The Mountforts fared much better, on the other hand, in Mrs. Behn's play, *The Emperor of the Moon*, in which they were Don Charmante, the Viceroy's nephew, who masquerades as the Prince of Thunderland, and his love Bellemante, the niece of Doctor Baliardo. In this excellent farce with spectacular trimmings, they played with the comedians Underhill as the moon-gazing doctor, Leigh as his man Scaramouch, Jevon as Harlequin, and Mrs. Corey as Mopsophil, the duenna.

IV

Whatever the cause, it is clear that writers of tragedy were not encouraged to produce for the United Company. In the five years following the performances of *The Duke of Guise*, only two new tragedies were added to the repertoire: Nat Lee's *Constantine the Great* and Rochester's posthumously acted version of *Valentinian*. How many revived tragedies were presented during the years from 1683 through 1687 it is impossible to say, but we do know that members of the royal family attended eighteen performances of tragedies chosen from the thirteen following: *Othello, Hamlet, Julius Caesar, Macbeth,* Tate's version of *King Lear, The Maid's Tragedy, Rollo, The Duchess of Malfi, All for Love, The Rival Queens, The Orphan,* Orrery's

Mustapha, and the second part of Crowne's *The Destruction of Jerusalem*.[1] In these years the company had given at least one new adaptation of a tragi-comedy, seven new comedies, four new farces, one new opera, and three new works designated by their authors as "plays"; and forty-one times the royal family had seen performances of twenty-six different comedies, tragi-comedies, or farces. The comparative lack of favor in which tragedy was held lasted some years, for in 1691 we find the complaint that the town will throng to a farce and "Hamlet *not bring Charges*."[2] The players themselves very likely had something to do with the matter, for John Crowne, in writing of how his *Darius* was received in the spring of 1688, remarks, "Nor do the present Company of Actors abound with Tragedians enow, to master that Humor. And they have no reason to contend with it, since they can please at a much cheaper rate, by Farce and Comedy."[3]

Under these circumstances the person who would make his bow as an author with a tragedy was unusually daring. Nevertheless, Mountfort was willing to venture, and he wrote *The Injur'd Lovers: or, The Ambitious Father*, which was acted at Drury Lane for the first time early in February, 1688.[4] In the prologue, which he himself delivered, he boldly announced:

1. They were also present at performances of *Valentinian* on February 11, 1684, and on May 16, 1687 (Nicoll, pp. 311, 313).
2. William Mountfort, *Greenwich Park* (London, 1691), Dedicatory Epistle.
3. John Crowne, *Darius* (London, 1688), Epistle Dedicatory.
4. Narcissus Luttrell's copy of the single leaf folio of the prologue and epilogue to *The Injur'd Lovers*, "*Printed for Sam Manship*, 1687," contains the owner's notation of the price and date of purchase, "1d., 6 Febr., 1687–88." It was advertised for sale by P. J. and A. E. Dobell in their catalogue No. 117 (1932). One would feel justified in assuming that February 6, 1688, was the date of the first performance of Mountfort's tragedy, were it not for the fact that *The*

JO Haynes's *Fate is now become my Share,*
For I'm a Poet, Married, *and a* Player:
The greatest of these Curses *is the* First;
As for the latter Two, *I know the* worst;

. . .

Some Care then must be taken, that may save
This Dear, *my First Begotten, from the Grave*:

. . .

Damn *it who will,* Damn *me, I'll write again*;
Clap down each Thought, nay, more than I can think,
Ruin my Family in Pen *and* Ink.
And tho' my Heart should burst to see your Spite,
True Talboy *to the last I'll Cry and Write,*
That's Certain.[1]

The first-begotten did not apparently survive long after birth. Gildon mentions that it "did not succeed as the Author wish'd";[2] and Langbaine was to echo the complaints of those who were dissatisfied with the action: "There are some *Surlyes*, who think that in this Play, Sir *Courtly writ for his Diversion, but never regarded Wit.*"[3] These fault-finders may have been in the mind of the woman who wrote some verses on Mountfort at the time of the presentation of *The Successful Strangers*:

May it succeed, and please the carping Age,
Who snarlingly enjoy'd thy Pucellage,

Double Marriage was given at Whitehall on that day (L.C. 5/148, p. 145 [Nicoll' p. 313]). It is possible, however, that *The Injur'd Lovers* was presented at the playhouse in the afternoon and that *The Double Marriage* was acted at court in the evening.

1. My quotations are from the first edition of the play, which has the following title-page: "The Injur'd Lovers; Or, The Ambitious Father. A Tragedy. Acted by Their Majesty's Servants at the Theatre Royal. By W. Mountfort, Com. Licensed, March 8. 1687/8. Ro. L'Estrange. London, Printed for Sam Manship at the Black Bull in Cornhill, MDCLXXXVIII."

2. *The Lives and Characters of the English Dramatick Poets* (London, 1698?), p. 102.

3. P. 378. Surly is the character who serves as a foil to Sir Courtly in Crowne's comedy.

As vext the first should so much pleasure give,
Foretelling that the next would longer live.

Possibly because of the limited opportunities he had had
in recent years to act in new tragedies, Betterton was
willing to assume the leading rôle, that of the brave general Rheusanes. His beloved Antelina was played by
Mrs. Bracegirdle, who was now appearing in the first part
that we may unquestionably associate with her name.[1]
The jealous and unfortunate Princess Oryala was allotted
to Mrs. Barry, and Mountfort himself essayed her unre-
quited lover Dorenalus. The lascivious King and the ambitious father Ghinotto, who together shared the responsi-
bility for the injuries to the lovers, were taken by Williams
and Griffin; the "old furious" Colonel, who is on the stage
in the fifth act only, was assigned to Sandford, and the
Soldiers whom he commands had Leigh, Jevon, Underhill,
and others as their impersonators.

The plot of the tragedy has as its center the infatuation
of the King of Sicily for Antelina, the daughter of Ghinotto.
She, however, is betrothed to the general Rheusanes, the
idol of the people. In order to dispose of his rival, the King
rewards the returning Rheusanes with the hand of his
sister, the princess Oryala, who is herself loved in silence
by the youthful Dorenalus, Ghinotto's son. When she becomes aware of the indifference of Rheusanes, Oryala is

1. I am aware of the fact that *The History of the English Stage* published by
Curll in 1741, p. 26, declares that Mrs. Bracegirdle "performed the Page in *The
Orphan*, at the Duke's Theatre in *Dorset-Garden*, before she was six Years old,"
and also that a "Miss Nanny" acted the part of Clita in D'Urfey's *A Common-
wealth of Women* (published in 1686). Mrs. Bracegirdle was one of the six
actresses admitted to the place and quality of "Comoedian in Ordinary" to
James II on January 12, 1688. It is worthy of note that Mrs. Mountfort and
Mrs. Corey were not among the six.

aroused to anger and threatens to see that Antelina shall dwell in everlasting solitude. The now jealous Dorenalus upbraids Rheusanes, only to be calmed by his friend and persuaded to make his sufferings known to Oryala; but when he is in her presence, he is unable to muster the necessary courage to declare his love. Rheusanes and Antelina agree to meet in the evening at a chapel outside the walls where the priest, during the shepherds' festival, will ratify their vows. Because of modesty, she would not have him behold her until the morrow; he agrees also not to speak to her until then. This conversation is overheard by Ghinotto, who reports it to the King. In the meantime, Oryala appeals to her brother to break off the match between her and Rheusanes, but he protests that he is forced to this act by state policy; whereupon she calls heaven to witness that she crosses her own desire to pleasure his.

At court on the next day, Rheusanes presents the bride, who, upon unveiling, proves to his great consternation to be Oryala. The King had compelled her to meet Rheusanes while Ghinotto, who is ambitious to have his daughter queen, had locked up Antelina. Dorenalus then turns upon the general and upbraids him for his perjury; but, after a stormy passage, the two friends become reconciled. Antelina also spurns Rheusanes when he attempts to address her, but she later regrets her act. Promising to prove the falsity of her lover, the King decoys her to his apartment, where, after ravishing her, he tells the truth concerning the trick that was played upon Rheusanes. When the general and the father realize what has been Antelina's lot, the three vow revenge. Dorenalus, at first, considers visiting his sister's fate upon Oryala; but he finally decides that he has no right to wrong her husband, who is his friend. As he is debating the matter with himself in the dark, he is mistaken by Rheusanes for the King and stabbed.

The action now moves rapidly to a close. The soldiers are ready to revolt in favor of their general. Oryala, when she sees that it is impossible for her duped husband to love her, stabs herself. Antelina pours poison into the wine which she and the King drink. After he returns from drawing up his guard to meet the rebellious soldiers, the King becomes mad and stabs Rheusanes and Ghinotto. He and Antelina die from the effects of the poison, and the Colonel commanding the revolting troops is left alive to bring the play to an end.

Although this tragedy is an ephemeral production, and there is no evidence that it was ever revived after its first performances, it does contain some scenes, which, if well acted, must have proved effective. The passage in the third act where the unhappy Rheusanes confronts in turn Dorenalus, Oryala, and Antelina may serve as an illustration. After his bride has been revealed and he is left alone, Dorenalus approaches him. Each of the men, hoping that he may be killed in the ensuing quarrel, taunts his erstwhile friend. Finally Rheusanes strikes Dorenalus, who draws, but soon afterwards throws him his sword, at which the general kneels and begs pardon for the blow. A reconciliation and parting follow. Oryala next appears. Rheusanes demands why she married him and is told of her love — that he was the only subject she could stoop to and that through her influence he won her brother's favor. She reminds him that she is his princess, but he replies that she is his wife, who has sold her freedom to a tyrant husband. These words arouse her resentment, and she vows she will have justice done her: she will die, but Antelina will be destroyed also. At last Antelina comes, and he kneels to her, but she draws away from him, curses him, and will not listen to his words, for the King awaits her. When music is heard, Rheusanes pulls himself together and leaves for the banquet.

The best-drawn of the characters is the proud and jealous Oryala, who is torn between her love for Rheusanes and her anger at being scorned by him, in vain hoping to win his affection and finally releasing him by suicide. Dorenalus, the part which Mountfort wrote for himself, is represented as young and impetuous, quick to become angry and equally quick to beg forgiveness. He is given to soliloquy, a laudable dramatic device when the author wishes the audience to know what ideas are running through the mind of his character, but apt to be clumsy when, as here, it is combined with any other purpose. The private communions of Dorenalus are twice overheard by others: Ghinotto listens while he talks of how he is cursed by love and questions him afterwards; and Rheusanes, mistaking him for the King, runs him through as he is telling himself that he will not harm the princess.[1] This listening to what is not intended to be heard is a stage-contrivance well-liked by Mountfort, for he also represents Ghinotto eavesdropping on the conversation between the lovers when they plan to meet at the shepherds' festival.[2]

Not much more need be said about the play. As a maiden effort at dramatic composition, it is by no means a work to be scorned, and is certainly no worse than the tragedies of Mountfort's fellow-player, George Powell. The lines, at their best, display a certain nervous energy:

1. Pp. 18–19, 49–50.
2. Pp. 13–14.

> Alas, Iv'e shaken hands with Hope long since,
> Have taken leave of Comfort; there's nothing
> That's related to Content but I have quarrel'd with.
> I have made a League with *Anguish* and *Despair*;
> The Devil drew the Articles, all Hell witnessed 'em,
> And I despise the malice of the Stars.[1]

At their worst, they do not fall beneath the level of some of the extravagancies of the heroic school:

> Thy *Antelina*, she shall be the Pile
> On which I'l burn, and as I burn I'l smile.[2]

Mention should also be made of the gracefully phrased lyric with which the play begins:

> Lucinda *Close or Veil your Eye,*
> *Where thousand Loves in Ambush lye;*
> *Where Darts are Pointed with such Skill,*
> *They're sure to Hurt, if not to Kill.*
> *Let Pity move thee to seem Blind,*
> *Lest Seeing, thou destroy Mankind.*

When *The Injur'd Lovers* was printed in 1688, it was by a curious twist of circumstance dedicated to James Douglas, Earl of Arran. In the epistle the author obsequiously craves his lordship's "kind Acceptance of this First Fruits of a *Young Muse*," and gives thanks for the many favors he has received from him and the noble family — that of Robert Spencer, Earl of Sunderland — to whom he is allied.[3] This Earl of Arran was in time to succeed to his father's title and become the fourth Duke of Hamilton, and many years later he was to be killed in a duel by the same Lord Mohun who accompanied Captain Richard Hill on the fatal December 9, 1692.

---

1. P. 27.   2. P. 33.
3. Lady Anne Spencer (1666–1690), the eldest daughter of Robert, Earl of Sunderland, was Arran's first wife.

V

After the conclusion of the action of *The Injur'd Lovers*, Jevon, who had taken the minor part of one of the soldiers, stepped forward and spoke the epilogue. Himself the author of a successful piece, he could properly beg those present to be charitable to the first venture of his fellow-player, who was then awaiting the verdict in the scene-room:

> *Pardon but this, and I will pawn my Life,*
> *His next shall match my* Devil *of a* Wife.
> *We'll grace it with Imbellishment of Song and Dance;*
> *We'll have the* Monsieur *once again from* France,
> *With's Hoope and Glasses, and when that is done,*
> *He shall Divert you with his* Riggadoone.

The promise was partially fulfilled, for Mountfort's next effort was graced with song and dance, but there is no indication in the published text that any Frenchman with hoop and glasses had a part. A bit of stage carpentry not published until 1697, the play was described on the title-page as *The Life and Death of Doctor Faustus, Made into a Farce . . . With the Humours of Harlequin and Scaramouche: As they were several times Acted by Mr. Lee and Mr. Jevon, at the Queens Theatre in Dorset Garden.*[1]

Farces, as has been noted, were among the most popular bits of dramatic fare during the period we are considering. When they or operas were given, the company used the house at Dorset Garden, now called the Queen's Theatre, which was better fitted than Drury Lane for performances needing elaborate scenes or stage-machinery. In recent

1. Otto Francke edited Mountfort's farce "mit Einleitung und Anmerkungen," Heilbronn (1886).

years three farces had had more than ordinary success:
Tate's *A Duke and no Duke*, Jevon's work just mentioned,
and Mrs. Behn's *The Emperor of the Moon*. When the first
of these was published in 1685 and again in 1693, the
author held in his prefaces that the business of farce was to
"exceed Nature and Probability" and that many works
styled comedies were near akin to farce. It appears also
that the writers from 1683 to 1688, when they designated
their plays as farces, had in mind the length as well and,
following Otway's example in *The Cheats of Scapin*, used
the three-act division instead of the conventional five of
comedy. In some instances farces utilized certain of the
spectacular and mechanical devices that were employed in
the productions of opera.

Marlowe's tragedy had been presented in London in
1662 when it was seen by Pepys at the Red Bull on
May 26, and also by Dr. Edward Browne at the Cockpit
in Drury Lane;[1] and in the following year a text was
printed "with New Additions as it is now Acted. With
several New Scenes." On September 28, 1675, King
Charles was present at a performance at the Duke's
Theatre.[2] In the same year Edward Phillips wrote in his
Theatrum Poetarum that "of all that [Marlowe] hath written to the Stage his Dr. *Faustus* hath made the greatest
noise with its Devils and such like Tragical sport."[3] It is
possible that the tragedy had been revived after the union,

1. Dr. Edward Browne's *Memorandum Book* (B.M. MS. Sloane 1900) contains a list of nine plays acted at the "Cock Pit in Drewry Lane" with the prices
paid for admission. The final entry is "Dr Fostus —— 1^s o Licens: Players."
Leslie Hotson, *The Commonwealth and Restoration Stage* (Cambridge, Massachusetts, 1928), p. 179, thinks the "licensed players" were undoubtedly the
company of George Jolly.

2. Nicoll, p. 310.

3. P. 25 of "The Modern Poets."

with Betterton as Faustus and Mountfort as Mephostophilis, for the names of these actors are written opposite
the parts in a copy of the 1663 edition.[1] It does not seem
likely that the notations could refer to the farce, for, although Mountfort might have appeared as Mephostopholis
in his version, it is hard to conceive of Betterton, who had
not acted in any other farces, consenting to pronounce the
abbreviated lines of Faustus in a play which was dom-
inated by Harlequin and Scaramouche.

If we dismiss Mountfort's farce with a shrug and the
statement that it is merely another striking example of
Restoration bad taste, we are pursuing the wrong course.
The story of Doctor Faustus permits two kinds of treatment. The approach may be philosophic and poetic,
stressing the doubts of the man zealous for knowledge before and after he has made his compact with the forces of
evil, his quest for power and beauty, and his inevitable
retribution; or the approach may be comic, accentuating
the tricks played by Faustus the magician. Marlowe em-
ploys both approaches. His Faustus is not only the poet
who would be made immortal by a kiss from Helen, but
also the sleight-of-hand performer who is able to turn the
courser's horse into straw. There is no indication that the
work of the Elizabethan was intended to move entirely
upon a lofty plane.

The additions made by the Restoration adapter belong
to the comic part of the action. From the original, but
with lines cut to the absolute minimum and with nearly
every bit of poetic beauty discarded, are kept the compact

1. In a copy in the British Museum, on the page containing the actors' names,
"Mr Baterton" is written opposite the part of Faustus and "Mr Munferd"
opposite that of Mephostophilis.

with Mephostopholis, the frequent giving of advice by the Good and the Bad Angels, the visit of Lucifer and Beelzebub and the summoning of the Seven Deadly Sins, the cheating of the Horse-Courser who pulls off Faustus' leg, the admonitions of the Old Man, the silencing of the Horse-Courser and the Carter, the summoning of the spirits of Alexander and Darius who fight before the Emperor, the tricking of Benvolio, the final moment of remorse before the doctor is dragged down to perdition, and the discovery of Faustus' limbs in his study.[1] Faustus and Mephostopholis, as they appear here, are the dry bones of Marlowe's creations, but enough of these characters and the scenes in which they take part was retained to make the title, *The Life and Death of Doctor Faustus*, a correct designation. The purpose of the adapter was not to convert an Elizabethan into a Restoration tragedy in the manner that Tate, Shadwell, and Dryden had transformed plays by Shakespeare, but to affix farcical materials to a work which already contained scenes of slapstick comedy.

Mountfort's innovation was the introduction of two figures from the *commedia dell' arte* who for several years had been well known to the theatregoer because of the frequent visits to London by Italian actors.[2] Probably the first Englishmen to play Scaramouche and Harlequin were Griffin and Haynes, who had, in 1677, appeared with the King's Company in Ravenscroft's comedy after the Italian manner which bore the unwieldy title of *Scaramouch a Philosopher, Harlequin a School-Boy, Bravo, Merchant, and Magician*. When Mrs. Behn's *The Emperor of the Moon*

---

1. See Appendix A.
2. See Nicoll, pp. 237–240, and Eleanore Boswell, *The Restoration Court Stage* (Cambridge, Massachusetts, 1932), pp. 118–125.

was presented ten years later, Griffin did not assume his
old rôle, but instead it was given to Leigh, and Harlequin
was taken by Jevon. In order that these two actors might
have a further opportunity to appear as these popular
characters a place was found for Scaramouche and Harlequin in Mountfort's farce.

As in *The Emperor of the Moon*, Scaramouche is the
doctor's man. For wages of forty crowns a year and plenty
to eat, he is willing to change one black art — his chimney-
sweeping trade — for another and to live with Faustus.
Harlequin, the discharged assistant to a mountebank, goes
to the magician's house and mistakes Scaramouche, who is
wearing his master's gown, for the doctor. Each is frightened by the other, Scaramouche thinking his visitor to be
the devil. After some horse-play, they lose their fear, and
Scaramouche promises Harlequin a devil that will swallow
a peck of his former master's turpentine pills a day. When
they are next seen, Scaramouche is conjuring from the
magic book. Mephostopholis responds and agrees to grant
them their desires. Harlequin demands food, drink, and a
handsome wench. A Giant comes, the upper and the lower
parts of his body separate and disappear, leaving a woman
in their place; but when the men try to kiss her, she
"*sinks*" amid flashes of lightning. Scaramouche knows
that they must not say grace at the devil's feast, but
Harlequin is always forgetting and bringing in the name
of the Deity. As a result the table flies into the air, and the
two are hoisted up to it, but upon Harlequin's promising
Mephostopholis "never to say Grace, or speak Proverb
more," they are let down. After a stag's head peeps from
the top of the pasty, birds fly out of the pot of fowl,
and the bread, bottles, and table disappear, the two are

caught fast in chairs, and, according to the direction which concludes the second act, several devils then enter, who "*black* Harlequin *and* Scaramouche'*s Faces, and then squirt Milk upon them. After the Dance they both sink.*" The last act takes place several years later. Scaramouche has left the doctor's service and become steward to a rich widow. As he is distributing doles to the poor, Harlequin is at hand in beggar's attire and nine times he takes the loaf and shilling which Scaramouche holds out. The poor people complain that they have had nothing, but they are beaten for their pains. Harlequin laughs at his cleverness until he hears sounds from the discontented persons who are returning; in order to escape them, he pretends to be hanging from a gibbet. Scaramouche reappears, and as he starts to read the paper which Harlequin has in one hand, the clever rascal slips a rope over him, hoists him up, and runs away. The tricked steward begs the poor people, who now surround him, to take him down. They do so, with the promise to have him hanged according to law, but, once on the ground, he trips up their heels and escapes.

This description of the scenes in which Leigh and Jevon figured makes it clear that the effectiveness must have depended more upon the agility of the actors and the efforts of the "machinist" than upon the lines of the dramatist. Many of the devices were well known. The ascendings and the sinkings had been utilized frequently in operas and such plays as Shadwell's *The Lancashire Witches*. The chair which traps a person sitting in it had found a place in Ravenscroft's *The Citizen turn'd Gentleman*,[1] and the

---

1. In Act III the country knight, Sir Simon Softhead, played by Underhill, when in the presence of Trickmore, disguised as a physician, sits down in a chair "*with arms, which locks him in that he cannot stir.*" Trickmore explains this as an "Italian device, we meant to surprise you with a rarity."

dividing Giant had appeared in the second part of *The Rover*.¹ The concluding episode of the farce, briefly described as "*Scene changes to Hell. Faustus Limbs come together. A Dance, and Song*," may have been suggested by the passage in *Dame Dobson*, where at the waving of a wand the parts of the body which had just fallen down the chimney "*approach and joyn together. The Body rises and walks to the middle of the Stage*." ²

Further comment would be superfluous. Largely a matter of pruning Marlowe's text and adding episodes in which physical action was prominent, Mountfort's task was probably the work of not more than two or three days. The adapter never saw fit to publish the farce during his lifetime, nor did he refer to it in any dedication, prologue, or epilogue subsequent to its performance. Whatever Mountfort's opinion may have been, the audience apparently liked his farce better than his tragedy, for it was revived five years after his death and again in 1724 at a time when *The Injur'd Lovers* had been long forgotten.³

VI

After our glance at Mountfort's first two attempts as dramatic author, we may again turn to his career as actor. On January 12, 1688, he was one of the twenty-two men and six women whom the lord chamberlain ordered to be sworn and admitted in the place and quality of "Comoedi-

---

1. Act III. Noted by John Genest, *Some Account of the English Stage* (Bath, 1832), I, 452.
2. Ravenscroft, *Dame Dobson* (London, 1684), p. 50. Noted by Genest, I, 453.
3. See Appendix B.

ans in Ordinary" to King James,[1] and before summer he played new parts in comedies by D'Urfey and Shadwell.

D'Urfey's *A Fool's Preferment, or The Three Dukes of Dunstable*, although "generally lik'd before the Acting," was opposed by the fraternity of basset-players, particularly by a "very great Lady" who was deeply offended,[2] and so the efforts of the well-disposed persons who came to the author's rescue were insufficient to save the day. The dramatist's purpose, as stated in the dedicatory epistle, was to compose a "wholsome Satyr" in order to oblige some country gentlemen or citizens of small estates, "whose Wives ne're heeding the approaching Ruin, took only care, they might have the Honour, to be seen at Play with Quality." A more obvious reason for writing the comedy, which is based on Fletcher's *The Noble Gentleman*, was that of preparing a suitable acting-medium for the comedians Nokes, Leigh, and Jevon, who were the three "dukes"— Cocklebrain, his uncle Justice Grub, and his servant Toby. Because Cocklebrain's wife Aurelia (played by Mrs. Boutell, who after several years' absence had returned to the theatre) finds it impossible to forego her beloved basset and retire to the country, some of her companions of the card table, the chief of them being Clermont (acted by Kynaston), pretend to her husband that they bring him the title of duke from the King, hoping thus to keep him in the city. He gloats over the honor, and his uncle, an avowed hater of the town, begins also to feel ambitious; but when he insists upon appearing in person before his tenants, Clermont and his friends take away the title, give it to Grub, and then remove it from the justice

1. L.C. 5/148, p. 66 (Nicoll, p. 298).
2. *Wit for Money: or Poet Stutter* (London, 1691), p. 26.

in order to bestow it upon Toby. At the end, the hoax is discovered, the dupers are punished, and Aurelia promises to atone for her past follies by showing the duty of a "most Penitent, Obedient Wife" and by no longer heeding "the senseless Fopperies of the Town." This combination of farcical situations and edifying conclusion did not, however, prevent the speedy interment of the play.

Etherege, to whom a copy of D'Urfey's comedy was sent, dismissed the work as "monstrous and insipid." [1] The first adjective might well apply to the episode of the dukes, the second to the subsidiary plot in which Mountfort assumed the leading character of Lyonel, the gentleman who "falls distracted" because he has been deprived of his love Celia by the King, and who also believes that the ruler intends to trap him for speaking treason. Allowed to wander at large, he falls upon the gamesters, beats Cocklebrain, and strips Toby of his clothes. The repentant and devoted Celia follows him, and at the end he is seized and taken away by the doctor, who presumably will effect his cure. What may have made this preposterous part attractive to an actor who sang a "clear Counter-tenour, and had a melodious, warbling Throat" was that Lyonel was required to sing several songs with music by Henry Purcell. Mountfort also delivered the epilogue, which D'Urfey alleges "was particularly carp'd at." The lines mention various types of madness and begin with words applying to the author of *The Injur'd Lovers*:

> 'Tis true, degrees of Madness all may fit, ⎫
> Some with too much, some with too little Wit, ⎬
> I have been Mad, or I should n'er have Writ. ⎭

---

1. Letter to the Duke of Buckingham, dated October 21, 1689 (Sybil Rosenfeld, *The Letterbook of Sir George Etherege* [Oxford, 1928], pp. 416–421).

The other occasion in the spring of 1688, when Mountfort stepped to the front of the stage and addressed the audience directly, proved to be very different from the unfortunate opening of *A Fool's Preferment*. He then spoke a prologue in which, after passing in review the various types of plays that had been popular (as rimed heroic tragedies, farces, and operas), he begged those who were ready to applaud or damn,

> *If all this stuff has not quite spoyl'd your taste,*
> *Pray let a Comedy once more be grac'd:*
> *Which does not Monsters represent, but Men,*
> *Conforming to the Rules of Master* Ben.

The work in question, *The Squire of Alsatia*,[1] which had been highly commended by those persons who had read the manuscript, brought back to the theatre as active playwright Thomas Shadwell, who after nearly seven years of silence was again ready to make a bid for popular approval.

It did not take the audience long to find that the author who in the past had pleased them with *The Sullen Lovers*, *Epsom Wells*, and *The Virtuoso* had lost none of his sense of what was diverting on the stage. In fact, *The Squire of Alsatia* was a blending of novelty and well-tried devices. It contained the old story of the unsophisticated country boy's coming to the city and being cheated by a group of sharpers, but freshness was added by placing the action in the notorious Whitefriars district and having the dwellers use their slang, which, in the words of the epilogue, had "*almost grown the language of the Town.*" It found a place also for the old plot of the contrasting points of view in training youth, but here the severe method is combined

1. See A. S. Borgman, *Thomas Shadwell: His Life and Comedies* (New York, 1928), pp. 75–78.

with a practical education in the country and the kindly method is joined with a liberal education at the university and the inns of court.

An expert at furnishing parts fitted to the abilities of the different actors, Shadwell did not fail to provide suitable rôles for the three comedians who had many times, in the old days of the Duke's Company, contributed to the success of his plays. The sides of the spectators were made to ache heartily with laughter by Leigh, who played the obstinate father with the uncontrollable temper, Sir William Belfond, in a manner which showed "a more spirited Variety" than Cibber ever "saw any Actor, in any one Character, come up to." The rustic boorish son who gave the title to the play was taken by Nokes, but he soon resigned the rôle to Jevon; and Underhill, when he acted the awkward servant Lolpoop, who speaks a north-country dialect, seemed to the author of the *Apology* "in the boobily Heaviness [of that character] . . . the immoveable Log he stood for!" The impudent Cheatly, the chief of the rascals who dupe the elder Belfond, was properly taken by that master of stage villains, Sandford; and Bowman, who had been musician in ordinary to Charles II, acted Truman, a part which required the singing of a Latin song, considered by Peregrine Bertie to be the only "extraordinary" thing in the play.

To Mountfort was assigned the part of the younger son who, after being constantly plagued by a discarded mistress and seducing an attorney's daughter, is finally "subdu'd to Marriage" and offers himself as a "Sacrifice without a blemish" to Isabella. Lively, witty, and often heartless, Belfond Junior — described by the author as a "man of Honour, and of excellent disposition and temper" —

gave Mountfort his first opportunity at acting a type of character that he was to make peculiarly his own. Admirers of *Sir Courtly Nice* would remember the amusing scenes between the fop and Surly as played by Mountfort and Griffin. In rôles of very different nature, these two actors were on the stage many times together in *The Squire of Alsatia*, for Griffin played the kindly disposed uncle, Sir Edward Belfond, a part in which Downes says he was not equaled by any of his successors. This wealthy merchant is willing to take a tolerant view of the follies of youth, to reason with his adopted son on matters of conduct, and, at the end, in a fit of righteous indignation to threaten to rout from Whitefriars the rogues who infest that district.

Shadwell expended his best strokes of characterization upon the men and, as a consequence, the women were slighted. Perhaps Lucia, the girl who falls a victim to the younger Belfond's charms,—a part played by Mrs. Bracegirdle, — is most clearly conceived. Mrs. Boutell, who was the heroine in *A Fool's Preferment*, had the longest female rôle as the furious and jealous Mrs. Termagant who is ceaseless in her efforts to be revenged upon her former lover. Mrs. Mountfort was Isabella, who, although called "Beautiful, and Witty to a Miracle," had slight opportunity from the lines allotted her to display her wit. Teresia, the cousin of Isabella, and Ruth, the "precise" governess of the young ladies, were taken by Mrs. Frances Maria Knight and the ever-ready Mrs. Corey respectively.

Anticipation of a new work by a popular dramatist who had had no plays produced for several years, satisfaction in seeing a comedy that gratified one's love for the old and the new, and delight that comes from excellent acting —

all combined to give *The Squire of Alsatia* a success unusual for that time. It had an initial run of thirteen perform-ances, and the receipts at the author's benefit on the third day were £130, the largest sum that had ever been re-ceived at Drury Lane when single prices were charged. On that occasion, vast numbers were turned away. Although not patronized by royalty, since King James could hardly be expected to look with favor upon the work of a former adherent of Shaftesbury, it was, nevertheless, well at-tended by the nobility, among whom Downes mentions especially Lord Jeffreys. That it was "often Honour'd" with his presence may have been partly due to an interest in the young actor who, a few years before, had delighted the chancellor and his table-companions by giving imita-tions of the leading lawyers of the day.

VII

After the spring productions of 1688 the annals of the theatre are silent for nearly a year. Probably the last ap-pearance of King James in a London playhouse was at the third day of Crowne's *Darius*, which had preceded Shad-well's comedy in time of performance. One might be justi-fied in inferring that *The Squire of Alsatia* from the pen of the leading Whig dramatist acted as harbinger of the tri-umph of James II's opponents. On the day that seems most likely to have been the time of its first presentation, May 4, the king issued his famous order that the declara-tion of indulgence should be read on two successive Sun-days in all churches in the kingdom. This affront to the clergy caused the protest of the seven bishops, their trial for libel, and subsequent acquittal amid much popular excitement. On June 10 a son and heir to the throne was born, an event which was followed shortly by the invitation to William of Orange from the leaders of both political parties, urging him to come to England and protect their liberties; and on November 5 William landed. Small wonder that matters of theatrical gossip were lost in speculations concerning those events which led to a change of crowns!

The name of Mountfort, however, is preserved among the records of scandal in a poem dealing with the birth of the prince. Because of the questions raised about whether or not the child was actually the offspring of the king and queen, James, on October 22, summoned to the Council chamber in Whitehall a group of persons who had been present at the birth to give depositions on the matter. Among them was Lord Jeffreys. An anonymous poetaster made this occasion the excuse for composing some verses called *The Deponents*,[1] in which he mentions the lord chancellor, his wife, and the actor:

1. On October 27, 1688, Jeffreys at the High Court of Chancery caused those who had been present at the birth to be sworn again after hearing read the depositions they had previously made. These depositions were published in a pamphlet entitled "The Several Declarations Together with the Several Depositions made in Council On *Monday*, the 22d of *October* 1688. Concerning the Birth of the Prince of Wales . . . *London*: Printed, and Sold by the Booksellers of *London* and *Westminster*." This pamphlet is available in *The Clarendon Historical Society's Reprints*, Series II (1884–1886), pp. 131–158. The poem, which is found in *Poems on Affairs of State, From 1640 to this present Year 1704*, III (1704), 258–265, was undoubtedly written with an open copy of "The Several Declarations" at hand. All those who deposed, with the exception of Colonel Edward Griffin, are mentioned; and they are introduced in the same order in which their depositions appear in the pamphlet. Humphry W. Woolrych, *Memoirs of the Life of Judge Jeffreys* (London, 1827), pp. 317–318, identifies "*M-fort*" with Mountfort. Later in the poem a "*M-ford*" is mentioned. Reference to the pamphlet makes clear that this person is John, Earl of Melfort.

> Then comes Great *George* of *England*, *Chancellour*,
> Who was with Expedition call'd to th' Labour:
> The Queen cry'd out as Women us'd to do,⎫
> And he believes the Prince is real too, ⎬
> But not so certain, nor 'tis fear'd so true ⎭
> As he wears Horns, that were by *M-fort* made;
> Them and his noise makes all the Fools afraid.

Whether these lines are more than idle chatter, it is impossible to say. But it should be noted that reports of this nature were not uncommon concerning Lady Jeffreys. At the time of the marriage of the young widow Lady Ann Jones to the lord chancellor, rumor had it that she was the mistress of Sir John Trevor.[1] It should be noted also that after the actor's death the attraction which Mountfort had exerted upon women was a matter of comment in both prose and verse.

Jeffreys did not have many days of power after he signed the deposition. Within two months, when his royal master's case was seen to be hopeless, he attempted to flee from England; but he was apprehended and sent to the Tower. There he died on April 18, 1689, just one week after the coronation of the new king and queen, and near the time when his former protégé, whose acting in *The Squire of Alsatia* he had watched on several occasions, was to play the leading rôle in another comedy by the same dramatist, now poet-laureate.

But before the presentation of Shadwell's *Bury Fair*, efforts had been made to disrupt the troupe. From the copy of a petition preserved in one of the warrant books of the lord chamberlain, we learn of the attempt on the part of Henry Killigrew to engage Leigh, Nokes, Mountfort,

---

1. Henry B. Irving, *The Life of Judge Jeffreys* (London, 1898), pp. 31-32.

Mrs. Corey, and others to withdraw from the company, and to act with him.[1] The half-brothers Killigrew, Henry and Charles, sons of the original patentee of the King's Company, were not apparently on good terms with each other. Henry, who was the elder, had, for instance, in a chancery suit alleged that he had been "much wronged and Injured by the secret and private Dealings" of Charles,[2] who had from the first been one of the joint directors of the United Company. Nursing resentment and feeling that he had not fared as well as he deserved at the union, he may have hoped to obtain a patent for a new company from the new rulers and may have persuaded some of the actors to come over to his fold. It appears that before he had gone very far, Charles Killigrew went to law and, pending the result of the suit, all those concerned in the engagement were readmitted to the playhouse except Mrs. Corey, who thereupon petitioned that she might be received with the others. An order to this effect was signed on March 11, 1689, as one of the first official acts of the new lord chamberlain, Charles Sackville, Earl of Dorset. Apparently nothing further resulted from Henry Killigrew's efforts.

A month or six weeks after Mrs. Corey was readmitted to the company, the former deserters from the playhouse joined with those who had remained loyal in presenting *Bury Fair*. There is nothing in this lively and, on the whole, entertaining comedy to indicate that it was composed during the eight months' painful illness of the author. Shadwell, ever on the alert for novelty, laid the

1. L.C. 5/149, p. 16. The petition was printed for the first time in a communication made by me to *The* [London] *Times Literary Supplement*, under date of December 27, 1934, and entitled "The Killigrews and Mrs. Corey."

2. Hotson, p. 263. For Henry and Charles Killigrew see Alfred Harbage, *Thomas Killigrew* (Philadelphia, 1930).

scene not in London but in Bury St. Edmunds, the town where he had attended school as a boy. Again he provided characters which were full-length portraits for the three principal comedians. Leigh was the French barber La Roch, who, like Mascarille, pretends to be a nobleman and thus causes a fluttering in the hearts of some of the affected provincial ladies. Nokes played the tiresome Sir Humphrey Noddy, a great lover of puns and practical jokes, whose antics are a source of continuous amusement to Mr. Oldwit, a professed "son of Ben" and an admirer of the good old days of acting at the Blackfriars. The latter rôle was taken by Underhill. To Bowman was also given a good part — that of Trim, who, although a beau and prone to indulge in high-flown conversation, surprizes all by proving not to be a coward. The women fared better than in Shadwell's comedy of the year before. Mrs. Corey and Mrs. Boutell were the two Fantasts, mother and daughter, who affect a fondness for French breeding and thus fall a prey to the pseudo-count. Mrs. Charlotte Butler, who won distinction as a singer and dancer as well as player, donned male attire to act the part of Oldwit's daughter who, under the name of Charles, serves Lord Bellamy, with whom she is in love. Although somewhat original in being represented as bored with London and as preferring his country estate where he may contemplate the works of nature and read the *Georgics*, his lordship is, in the main, a rather heavy character, and the action is likely to lag when he holds the center of the stage. Despite the fact that it was secondary in importance to the characters assumed by Mountfort and Leigh, Bellamy was taken by Betterton.

The Mountforts, who had played opposite each other as lovers in *The Emperor of the Moon* and *The Squire of Al-*

satia, were to do so again as Wildish and Gertrude. The former, who scorns to be called a wit because so many pretenders have usurped the title, is the moving spirit in the stratagem of the masquerading barber. A city man, he cannot understand his friend Bellamy's preference for the country; and in his pursuit of Gertrude he has many a merry tilt. This is such a part as Cibber had in mind when he praised Mountfort for giving the truest life

to what we call the *Fine Gentleman*; his Spirit shone the brighter for being polish'd with Decency: In Scenes of Gaiety, he never broke into the Regard that was due to the Presence of equal or superior Characters, tho' inferior Actors play'd them; he fill'd the Stage, not by elbowing and crossing it before others, or disconcerting their Action, but by surpassing them in true masterly Touches of Nature. He never laugh'd at his own Jest, unless the Point of his Raillery upon another requir'd it. — He had a particular Talent in giving Life to *bons Mots* and *Repartees*: The Wit of the Poet seem'd always to come from him *extempore*, and sharpen'd into more Wit from his brilliant manner of delivering it; he had himself a good Share of it, or what is equal to it, so lively a Pleasantness of Humour, that when either of these fell into his Hands upon the Stage, he wantoned with them to the highest Delight of his Auditors.

Mrs. Mountfort, who was "Mistress of more variety of Humour" than Cibber ever knew in any one actress, and who was notable for her vivacity, played in *Bury Fair* the woman of common sense who is wearied by the affectations of the Fantasts. Although her father would have her marry Bellamy, she affirms that she is a free heiress of England and is therefore resolved to choose for herself. But after making the most of several opportunities to banter with Wildish, she finally decides to dissemble no longer and to give him her hand.

Soon after acting Shadwell's comedy, in which Mount-fort had spoken the prologue and Mrs. Mountfort the epilogue, the company presented *The Fortune Hunters, or Two Fools well met* with husband and wife again in the leading parts. In this play, concerning which the author James Carlisle, an actor turned soldier, says *"without Wit he sets up for a Poet,"* [1] Mountfort played Young Wealthy, a Londoner on bad terms with his country father Sir William, who considers him the "Debauch of the Town." He is kept by Lady Sly and cuckolds the Exchange-man, Mr. Spruce; then he falls in love with Maria. This young heiress, who was acted by his wife, is of a lively nature and would let the first young gentleman that she likes have the spending of her estate. At the Exchange she meets Young Wealthy, and the two have a witty passage at arms until they are interrupted by Lady Sly in disguise. Surmising who the intruder is, Maria arouses the widow's jealousy by showing a letter which she pretends was sent by the man with whom she talked. After he has fought in a duel and been thrust into prison for debt by Maria, who wishes to test him, the young lady, now disguised as a man, goes to him, pretending to be brother to the person with whom he fought, and offers him his freedom provided he will again meet his rival alone within a half-hour. Arriving at the rendezvous, he is told that his opponent's arm is disabled and that the brother will be substitute. But he soon dis-covers that his visitor is no less a person than his love, and the ending is what one expects.

Although the rôles taken by the Mountforts carry the play, the two Leighs, Nokes, and Mrs. Knight were also well-equipped. Leigh was the father, Sir William Wealthy,

1. Prologue.

who would fain marry Maria and act the young blood of twenty. Angered with his son at the beginning, he at one time is ready to fight him when he thinks him a rival; but after he has been outwitted, he bestows his blessing. Nokes naturally was the Exchange-man Spruce, who is so afraid of being thought jealous that he does everything possible to procure himself a pair of horns. He takes Young Wealthy to his wife, and feels no anger when he finds the two kissing. His clever and ambitious spouse, who would have him an alderman, and who is able to do with him as she wishes by using a goodly amount of flattery and by pretending to be jealous, was played by Mrs. Knight. Mrs. Leigh, who had taken the amorous Aunt to Mountfort's Sir Courtly, again acted the older woman pursuing a younger lover in the part of the widowed Lady Sly. Although pretending to have a great care for her reputation, she actually keeps Young Wealthy, and, fearful of losing him, she is easily made jealous by Maria and further arouses Sir William against him.

Royalty did not patronize either of these two diverting comedies. Queen Mary's first appearance at the theatre was at a revival of *The Spanish Friar* on May 28, 1689.[1] Dryden's play, which had been banned by her father on December 8, 1686,[2] was not an inspired choice. A record of what happened on that occasion has been preserved in a frequently quoted letter attributed to Daniel Finch, Earl of Nottingham,[3] which tells how the "only day her Majesty gave herself the diversion of a play and that on which she designed to see another, has furnished the town

1. L.C. 5/149, p. 368 (Nicoll, p. 314).
2. L.C. 5/147, p. 239 (Nicoll, p. 10).
3. Printed on pp. 78–80 of "Appendix . . . Part the Second" in vol. II of Sir John Dalrymple, *Memoirs of Great Britain and Ireland* (2d ed., London, 1773).

with discourse for near a month." Certain expressions making mention of a usurping queen were thought by some of the people in the pit to be appropriate to Her Majesty, and so they watched her as she sat embarrassed in her box, holding her fan up to her face, and frequently looking behind her to call for her palatine and hood. The awkward situation gave the town material for conversation until, to continue quoting from the letter, "something else happened which gave as much occasion of discourse; for another play being ordered to be acted, the q—— came not, being taken up with other diversion." The play, which she ordered to be performed but which she did not care to attend, was *Sir Courtly Nice* "Acted by the Queenes Command" on May 31.[1]

Thus Mountfort, who was to become the favorite actor of Queen Mary, was prevented from appearing before royalty until November, when he took the part of the King in *The Massacre of Paris*. For some time during the intervening months, if the words in a prologue are to be taken literally, he had emulated his former associates, Carlisle and Wiltshire, and become a soldier. At the time of the acting of *Bury Fair*, many of the frequenters of the theatre had gone or were preparing to go to Ireland or the Continent to fight against James and Louis, for the epilogue states,

> Most of our constant Friends have left the Town,
> Bravely to serve their King and Country gone.
> Our unfrequented Theatre must mourn,
> Till the Brave Youths Triumphantly return.

Mountfort's brief military experience, if we have a right to assume that he went to Ireland, was in the army of Schom-

1. L.C. 5/149, p. 368 (Nicoll, p. 314).

berg, William III's second-in-command. The troops, which consisted of a few experienced Dutch and French soldiers and a large number of untrained English peasants under the leadership of raw officers, set sail for Ireland in August and entrenched themselves at Dundalk early in September. Terrible hardships followed. Some of the Frenchmen proved traitors, and much sickness prevailed. For several weeks Schomberg, with his comparatively small and undisciplined force, faced a larger army of the enemy until in November the Irish retired to winter quarters. But before that time, Mountfort — if in deed he had been with the army in Ireland — had returned to England, for on October 15 [1] he and other members of the company were summoned to be at the office of the lord chamberlain on Friday morning, October 18, when the controversy growing from "Mr Haynes complaineing against Mr Montfort" was to be heard.

We may consider, then, that sometime during October he delivered "*A Prologue spoken by Mr. Mountfort, after he came from the Army, and Acted on the Stage,*" which I quote in its entirety:

> As reading of Romances did inspire
> The fierce *Don Quixot* with a Martial Fire;
> So some do think by acting *Alexander*,
> Gave me the whim of being a Commander.
> But then Reflecting that *I* had left behind me,
> An Audience rudely, that had us'd me kindly,
> My Conscience of Ingratitude accus'd me,
> Bid me return, where you too well had us'd me
> Ask pardon, and it should not be refus'd me.
> Thus relying on your Mercy *I* am come,
> Leaving *Dundalk*, to Act with you at Home.

1. L.C. 5/192 (Nicoll, p. 299).

> Forgive me then, and in return I'll swear,
> Ever to be your most Obedient Player.[1]

The foregoing words, in addition to referring to his presence at Dundalk, also indicate that by this time he had added the hero of *The Rival Queens* to his repertoire of parts.

Despite its extravagancies, mad Nat Lee's Alexander is one of the most famous rôles in the history of the English stage, and for nearly a century and a half it made its appeal to tragedians. Originally acted by Hart in the spring of 1677, it was later taken by Scum Goodman, who, when he was in the good graces of the Duchess of Cleveland, would play the part only upon the assurance that she would be present at the theatre.[2] After the union of the companies, Alexander passed to Betterton, who appeared as the world-conqueror for a few years — at least until December, 1685,[3] but very likely much longer. Then, tiring of Lee's hero, he relinquished the rôle to Mountfort, who made it his own and acted it until the time of his death.

The actor who takes this part has an opportunity to run the gamut of the passions from fury to tenderness. Extremely violent, Alexander on one occasion is ready to burst unless he is given leave to rave awhile; on another, he throws himself weeping by the body of his truest friend Clytus, whom he has just killed. Presumably Mountfort was at his best in the scenes in which the warrior appears as lover. It was of such acting that Cibber was to write:

1. *Poems on Affairs of State*, 5th ed., (1703), I, ii, 238.
2. Thomas Davies, *Dramatic Miscellanies* (London, 1784), II, 240.
3. A warrant dated December 19, 1685, orders that £20 "be paid unto Mr Baterton . . . for the King & Queenes Maties Seeing the play called Alexander at the Theatre Royall." L.C. 5/147, p. 52 (Nicoll, p. 318).

In Tragedy he was the most affecting Lover within my Memory. His Addresses had a resistless Recommendation from the very Tone of his Voice, which gave his Words such Softness that, as *Dryden* says,

> —— *Like Flakes of feather'd Snow,*
> *They melted as they fell!*

All this he particularly verify'd in that Scene of *Alexander*, where the Heroe throws himself at the Feet of *Statira* for Pardon of his past Infidelities. There we saw the Great, the Tender, the Penitent, the Despairing, the Transported, and the Amiable, in the highest Perfection.

His Statira was probably at first Mrs. Boutell, the creator of the part, and later Mrs. Bracegirdle. Described as "all softness, all melting, mild, and calm as a rock'd Infant," she decides to take leave of mankind because of the report of Alexander's love for Roxana; but in a powerful scene in which her rival taunts her, she is finally aroused to change her resolve and see her husband. It is the passage which follows to which Cibber refers. The rôle of the other queen, Roxana, originally acted by Mrs. Marshall, was at this time probably played by Mrs. Barry. This tempestuously jealous woman, who had been an adept at riding and hunting before she captured the man admired by all the world, cannot see him taken away by the puny daughter of Darius. When Alexander ignores her threats, she cries that she could tear his flesh or all the world to pieces; and after killing Statira, she faces the man she loves in spite of his cruelties and appeals to him in the name of their unborn child. He is touched and forgives her for the murder, but will not take her back; whereupon she departs, calling on an avenger for her wrongs. Despite the frequent rant and fury of the lines, these scenes must have been most effective in the theatre, especially when Alexander and the two queens were in the hands of Will Mountfort, Elizabeth Barry, and Anne Bracegirdle.

VIII

In the latter part of 1689, plays were given at Drury Lane by each of the two writers who seven years before had joined pens in *The Duke of Guise*. Although Nat Lee wrote *The Massacre of Paris* as early as 1679,[1] his tragedy had to wait ten years for production; in the meantime, some of its lines had done service in his collaborative venture with Dryden. The massacre was, of course, that of St. Bartholomew's Eve. It was evident that a play containing anti-Catholic sentiments would not be displeasing to a people who within the year had caused a Catholic sovereign to flee and who now felt that for the future there would be a Protestant upon the throne. It is worthy of notice that the first play seen by Queen Mary after the ill-advised performance of *The Spanish Friar* was this tragedy, which she and the maids of honor attended on November 7.[2] As speaker of the prologue, Mountfort, whose opportunity to act before royalty in May had been thwarted, now made his first bow to the queen.

The principal rôle, that of Admiral Coligny, the aged Protestant leader, was taken by Betterton, whose wife appeared for the first time since the union of the companies in a new part as the bloody and domineering queen mother, Catherine de' Medici. Williams was the ambitious and vengeful Duke of Guise, and Mrs. Barry, the unfor-

1. See Roswell Ham, *Otway and Lee* (New Haven, 1931), pp. 165–167.
2. L.C. 5/149, p. 368 (Nicoll, p. 314).

tunate Marguerite, who, despite loving Guise, is forced
against her will to wed Henry of Navarre. Mountfort
acted the weak king, Charles IX. Although he hates con-
spiracies and treachery, Charles is so completely under his
mother's influence that he plays the coldly calculating
villain. He acts with energy in persuading Guise to re-
nounce Marguerite and with cruelty when he gives orders
to have his reluctant sister dragged to the King of Navarre. He dissembles friendship, softness, and pity when
in the presence of the Admiral. At the end, however, he
is filled with horror and, as his dying counsel, begs Catherine to stop the vast murder they have begun. The part
of weakness forced to masquerade as strength is somewhat
different from Mountfort's previous impersonations.

But in Dryden's tragedy, presented in December,
Mountfort had returned to a congenial type of rôle.[1]
Dryden, whose last dramatic work had been the opera
Albion and Albanius, unfortunately presented at the time
of Monmouth's rebellion and therefore a financial failure,
had by now lost the offices which he had held under
Charles II and James II, and against his will was once
more forced to write for the stage. The Earl of Dorset, to
whom the last two comedies by Thomas Shadwell had
been dedicated, had read *Don Sebastian* in manuscript and
had sent word to the dramatist that in this tragedy he had
written beyond any of his former plays. One cannot help
feeling that Dryden, who was now writing primarily for
the means of livelihood, had determined on a dramatic

1. In the 1690 edition of *Don Sebastian*, the parts of both Dorax and Don
Antonio are given to Betterton. The mistake is corrected in the edition of
1692, where "Mr. *Montford*" stands opposite the rôle of Don Antonio.

vehicle which would give as many of the company as possible the opportunities for displaying their peculiar gifts. The leading part, the disillusioned Dorax, who although a renegade has retained his nobility of character, naturally fell to Betterton, and Williams played the brave and generous Don Sebastian, the captive king of Portugal, who with Dorax shares the great moment of the play — another of those moving confrontation scenes which Dryden was at his best in writing. Mrs. Barry displayed both pride and tenderness as the unfortunate queen, Almeyda, who repulses the Emperor of Barbary and learns at the end that her husband Don Sebastian is also her brother. An adept at presenting tyrants, Kynaston as the Emperor Muley–Moloch assumed "a fierce, Lion-like Majesty in his Port and Utterance that gave the Spectator a kind of trembling Admiration"; and Sandford, we may assume, did all that was expected of a villain as Benducar, the treacherous and ambitious chief minister, who attempts to poison Dorax and who kills the Emperor during the uprising.

Although the principal action contained enough material for a full-length play, the author could not resist introducing a humorous subplot in order to make use of the talents of the comedians. And so for Mountfort were written the lines of the young and noble Don Antonio, who is described as "the wittiest Womans toy in *Portugal*," and whose general attitude is expressed in the statement, "Pleasure has been the bus'ness of my life." Made prisoner in the war, he is taken to the slave-market, where he is bridled and put through his paces, by Mustapha, the "Captain of the Rabble," played by Leigh. The Mufti Abdalla, acted by Underhill, purchases the young man and brings him home as a slave to his wife Johayma — Mrs. Leigh, of course! Here he sees and falls in love with the Mufti's daughter, Morayma — Mrs. Mountfort, to be sure! What follows is inevitable. Johayma will, like the Aunt in *Sir Courtly Nice* or Lady Sly, attempt to force her attentions upon the younger man; Morayma and Antonio, as Gertrude and Wildish or Maria and Young Wealthy, will have some passages of brisk talk; and finally, after becoming involved in difficulties, the lovers will outwit the older man and woman.

The scenes in which they appear in the third and fourth acts are highly amusing. In the dark Antonio mistakes the wife for the daughter, with whom he has an appointment, and addresses her by the daughter's name, but upon discovering his error, pretends that he thought she was called Morayma. When she becomes too aggressive in her love-making, he feigns to have qualms of conscience, at which she turns upon him and calls for help, while he plays loudly on the flute in a vain attempt to drown her cries. The Mufti, who has been aroused, then appears in his nightgown, and it looks as if the slave would fare badly; but when he promises to do anything for her if she will speak the truth, Johayma, taking what she believes to be a hint, tells her husband how she heard music in the garden and came down to prevent Antonio from alluring any of the female slaves. The Mufti is, however, not entirely convinced. After the others have left, Morayma, who has been in the arbor all the time, comes forth to Antonio and jokes at his expense. He makes love, but she keeps him at arm's length until finally she allows him a kiss. They agree to meet on the morrow at the same hour; but at that time the suspicious Mufti is at hand disguised as a slave.

Thinking him Antonio, Morayma hands him a casket of jewels. Upon recognizing her father, she makes the best of the situation by saying that the contents represent the spoil of orphans and she will not be the possessor of what he has stolen. Unfortunately Antonio then enters richly dressed and assumes that the person in slave's habit has the horses in charge. The Mufti realizes the truth and threatens to call, but is forcibly silenced. To add to the difficulties, Johayma looks down from the balcony, and, seeing Antonio with a woman, arouses the servants. All is confusion. Morayma tells her lover to flee with the jewels, but he will not take them without her. After the Mufti has snatched them, she calls out that they have been stolen by a lusty rogue. The servants then seize their disguised master and give him a good beating as she escapes with the casket.

These passages of hilarious and boisterous comedy form the greatest possible contrast to the serious plot of the play, which is of course uppermost in the concluding scenes. After Betterton as Dorax had pronounced the moral, which brought the fifth act to an end, the two Mountforts again came to the fore and spoke a somewhat risqué epilogue. One cannot help wondering whether Dryden, after seeing Antonio and Morayma played by Will and Susanna Mountfort, may not have thought that the pair for whom he wrote Celadon and Florimel twenty years before, Charles Hart and Nell Gwynn, had found worthy successors.[1]

1. It has been suggested by Mr. Montague Summers in his edition of *Dryden The Dramatic Works* (London, 1931), II, 5, that "Mountfort, no doubt, played Celadon when *Secret Love* was given at Whitehall before James II on Friday, 15 December, 1686." The statement may be correct, but there is no contemporary reference to Mountfort's appearing in that rôle. Summers (III, 184) also holds

IX

Not long after the first performances of Dryden's trag-edy, Mountfort had his third play ready for production. Styled a tragi-comedy by the author, *The Successful Strangers* [1] was introduced to the audience at Drury Lane by a prologue spoken by Mrs. Bracegirdle in which she begs indulgence for her fellow-actor:

> *Well, worthy Auditors, I am come again,*
> *To plead in the behalf of a weak Pen;*
> *Quaking within the expecting wretch does sit,*
> *To hear the dreadful sentence of the Pit.*
> *Some are resolv'd (he hears) it shall be damn'd,*
> *Only because 'tis from a Players hand;*
>
> .   .   .
>
> *Cou'd but the Females see, how very sad*
> *He looks, they'd pitty such a likely Lad,*
> *But hang him slave, he's married, there's the curse,*
> *Ah Devil for this better and for worse.*

---

that Mountfort acted in another of Dryden's comedies, and quotes W. R. Chet-wood, *A General History of the Stage* (London, 1749), p. 235: "The first Part he [i.e. Robert Wilks] performed of *Mountford*'s was *Palamede* in *Dryden*'s *Marriage Alamode*." But Cibber, who is a better authority than Chetwood on Mountfort, states definitely (*Apology*, ed. Lowe, I, 237): "Upon his [i.e. Wilks'] first Arrival, *Powel*, who was now in Possession of all the chief Parts of *Monfort*, and the only Actor that stood in *Wilks*'s way, in seeming Civility offer'd him his choice of whatever he thought fit to make his first Appearance in; though, in reality, the Favour was intended to hurt him. But *Wilks* rightly judg'd it more modest to accept only of a Part of *Powel*'s, and which *Monfort* had never acted, that of *Palamede* in *Dryden*'s *Marriage Alamode*."

1. My quotations from the play are based upon the first edition, which has as title-page: "The Successfull Straingers, A Trage-Comedy: Acted by their Majesties Servants, At the Theatre Royal, Written by William Mountfort. Licensed and Entred according to Order. London, Printed for James Black-well, at Bernards-Inn-Gate, Holbourn; and Sold by Randal Taylor near Sta-tioners-Hall. 1690." In the text I spell the title in the modern form.

Well Gallants, be impartial to him this day,
If his Play's bad, damn him indeed I say;
But if by chance, he has writ it to your mind,
As ever you expect my heart to find
Inclinable to you, be kind to him,
And Ladies if you smile, we doubt not them.

Although the dramatist in his preface was to protest that he was no scholar and therefore "*Incapable of stealing from Greek and Latin Authors, as the better Learned have done,*" he neglected to note the fact, soon to be recorded by Langbaine, that in *The Successful Strangers* he was "beholding to others for part of his Plot; he having made use of *Scarron*'s Novel, call'd *The Rival Brothers*, in working up the Catastrophe of his Comedy." [1]

The contents of *Les deux frères rivaux*, which is the nineteenth chapter of the second part of *Le Roman Comique*, may be summarized briefly. One day a stranger in Seville, Dom Sanche de Sylva, addresses a young lady, Dorothée de Montsalve, in church. Although he informs her that he is the son of the governor of Quito and has spent some part of his life with the army in Flanders, she will neither tell him her name nor do more than assure him that she is of the quality and that her face will not frighten him. But as a result of this conversation, the two fall in love. Dom Sanche is overjoyed to receive a letter one morning asking him to accompany the bearer that evening. He is, of course, taken to his fair acquaintance. The lovers have several such meetings until word reaches the ears of one

---

1. P. 379. Langbaine also says, "Had I been of the number of his Friends, I should have endeavour'd to have perswaded him still to act *Sir Courtly Nice*, in bestowing only *Garniture* on a Play (as he calls it) as a *Song* or a *Prologue*, and let alone fine Language, as belonging only to *Pedants* and poor Fellows, that live by their Wits."

of her admirers, Dom Diegue, whose *valet de chambre*, Gusman, has learned from Isabelle, Dorothée's maid, of her mistress's intrigue. This rival dresses as a beggar and spies upon the others. Finally, with the assistance of two assassins, he attacks Dom Sanche, but the stranger proves the better fighter and gives him his death wound. To escape the law, Dom Sanche retires to a convent, a place to which Dorothée, pretending devotion, later repairs.

The lovers vow eternal constancy, and then Dom Sanche makes his way to Naples and serves in warfare against the Algerines. After showing great bravery in a sea-fight, he jumps overboard in order to escape capture and, by hard swimming, succeeds in reaching Sicily. Here he suffers a severe illness and allows the word to go forth that he is dead. In a fisher's garb he proceeds to the house of the Marquis Fabio, whom he had known in Flanders. There he is well received by his friend, and in time the two set out for Seville.

The news of his death had reached Peru and caused his father to die of the shock. His brother, Dom Juan, was left 400,000 écus on condition that, if the report should prove false, he should refund half to Dom Sanche. Dom Juan then went on his travels and arrived in Seville, where he fell in love with Dorothée. Her father would be happy to see her speedily wed, but she of course can think of no one but Dom Sanche. Her sister Féliciane, however, loves the visitor from the New World; and Dorothée, in order to help her, has Isabelle seek out Dom Juan and direct him to come to the garden at midnight. It happens that about this hour Dom Sanche and the Marquis Fabio, who have now arrived at Seville and have heard of Dorothée's suitor, become involved in a quarrel with some armed men. In the ensuing sword-play, Dom Sanche receives a slight wound, but he repays his adversary with an ugly thrust. Then as he is fleeing, he runs into Dom Manuel, who is returning home from a neighbor's and entering his garden. He is given sanctuary and hidden among the laurel trees. Isabelle appears and, mistaking him for Dom Juan, is ready to conduct him to Dorothée. A series of misunderstandings follows in rapid order: Dom Juan arrives, and Dom Manuel takes him to a place where he need not fear being recognized; Dorothée thinks Dom Sanche a ghost and swoons at his appearance; Dom Sanche reproaches her with inconstancy; the watch clamors for admittance to arrest the person who has been fighting in the streets; Dom Manuel discovers that Dom Juan is a man of wealth and resolves not to let him out of the house until he marries one of the daughters; the rival brothers draw their swords, but are prevented from fighting by Dom Manuel; and finally they recognize each other. All ends well with three weddings on the same day. Dorothée is married to Dom Sanche and Féliciane to Dom Juan. The Marquis Fabio becomes the husband of the cousin and heir of Dom Diegue, and thus brings to an end the enmity of that family with Dom Sanche.

In his adaptation of this narrative to the dramatic form, Mountfort, who probably used the English translation,[1]

1. He may have used the English translation by J. B., printed in 1665 for "*John Playfere*, at the *White Lion* in the Upper-walk of the New Exchange: and *William Crooke*, at the *Three Bibles* on *Fleet-Bridge*," with the title: "The Comical Romance: or A Facetious History of a Company of Stage-Players. Interwoven with divers Choice Novels, Rare Adventures, and Amorous Intrigues. Written Originally in *French* by the Renowned Scarron." The same version of *The Rival Brothers* that appeared in this volume was reprinted in a translation of *The Comical Romance*, printed by "*J.C.* for *William Crooke*, at the Greendragon without *Temple-bar*. 1676."

in no place copies Scarron's language verbatim. He makes numerous departures from the original and adds scenes and touches of characterization, several of which were undoubtedly due to the personnel of the acting company. He and Powell were the brothers and strangers, now called Silvio and Antonio, but not rivals as in the French story. The two sisters, Dorothea and Feliciana, retain the names given them by Scarron. Feliciana is made a more vivacious figure than her prototype and has some scenes of bantering with Antonio. Needless to say, this part was written for Mrs. Mountfort, whereas Mrs. Knight played Dorothea. The father Dom Manuel becomes the lewd Don Lopez, and is made a comic figure for Nokes. Silvio's rival for the hand of Dorothea, Dom Diegue, is called Don Carlos. Acted by Williams, he is presented as haughty and ready to seek vengeance, but he is not killed in the encounter with Silvio, and at the end is satisfied to seek his happiness elsewhere than at the hands of Dorothea.

The author's principal addition to the *dramatis personae* was in providing Don Carlos with a father, Don Francisco, again a comic rôle. The scenes in which he and Don Lopez haggle over the marriage terms for their children, quarrel, and become reconciled only to quarrel again, are exceedingly amusing. Of course this character was introduced to give the audience the pleasure of seeing Anthony Leigh once more share scenes of laughter with Nokes. Dorothea's woman, Isabelle, becomes the amorous Farmosa, an almost farcical part for Mrs. Corey. Gusman, the *valet de chambre* to Dom Diegue, retains the same name: in each work he loves Dorothea's woman, but in the play the action in which he takes part is entirely humorous, both in the scenes in which he makes love to Farmosa and in the episode, after he has been wounded, when he vents his anger at the surgeon. This character was made for Cave Underhill. The hero's valet Sanchez becomes a different person as the Englishman Sancho, played by William Bowen, who in the end is to be married to Farmosa. For Mrs. Bracegirdle was written a comparatively insignificant part which corresponds to no character in the narrative, Biancha, who marries Don Carlos. Other minor figures added were Biancha's father, Don Pedro, played by George Bright, and his niece, acted by Mrs. Miles.

The scene of the play is laid entirely in Seville, and the action, instead of covering considerably more than a year, is compressed within a few days. The hero, as in the French source, meets the heroine at the church, but he does not kill his man and so is not forced to flee from the country. The concluding semi-farcical scenes in the garden and the house were suggested by Scarron's narrative, although there are necessarily numerous changes and omissions. In both instances, however, the hero, after fighting, meets the father of his love and is allowed to have sanctuary in the garden; the brother on the same night is given a key to the garden and enters shortly after the hero; the servant comes to conduct Dom Juan–Antonio within the house and leads Dom Sanche–Silvio instead; the father returns later and, thinking the person in hiding to be the one to whom he gave refuge, takes him inside; the brothers confront each other, and at the end are satisfactorily paired with the young ladies of their choice.

At the conclusion of the play, Leigh and Nokes stepped forth to speak the epilogue, pulling the supposedly reluctant author with them. They beg him to bear up and be not shy; he makes his bow to the audience and leaves.

Then Nokes appears to be in a quandary about what to say:

Theres one thing I'm sure, which none of you know,

Leigh interrupts: "*Yes they do; that is, the Play's but so so.*" And then Nokes continues:

Well, mark what I say, and remember it too,
Mr. Lee *and my self — come* Tony *let's go.*

In this unexpected manner the performance was brought to a close.

The play was without doubt successful, and Mountfort was not displeased with its reception, for he was to say in the preface that the "*Masters of the Play-house lost nothing by it*" and to hope that the "*Town will be as kind to [his] next third day, as they were to [his] last.*" We learn from an entry in one of the warrant books of the lord chamberlain that Queen Mary was present at a performance of this comedy. On July 24, 1690, Sir Rowland Gwyn, treasurer of Their Majesties Chamber, was directed to "pay or cause to be paid unto William Montfort the sum of ten pounds for the play called the Successfull Strangers acted before Her Matie the said sume being assigned by the Comoedians to be received by him." [1]

The player-dramatist found an opportunity to speak well of the new government by representing Antonio as having recently been in England. To the question how that country thrives, he replies: "'tis in a fairer way then ever, the Prince and the People have faith in Each other, and there's great hopes that *Brittain* will retreive its

---

1. L.C. 5/150, p. 123. The warrant is unsigned, and it is therefore possible that the money was never paid.

long lost glory." Don Lopez also, although he is a Catholic, wishes well to the land across the channel:

> May that Countrey, its Trade nor its Church never loose,
> May they stand by their Prince, and he Conquer their Foes,
> And the Wives go as fine as they will in their Cloaths.[1]

Possibly it was words such as these which caused an adherent of James to send Mountfort some fault-finding verses, in which the playwright is censured because "with little wit and much ill Nature [he] set up for Comedy and Satyr":

> Prithy be free thou lucky Rogue,
> How came thy Jests so much in vogue,
> That 'tis a mode to laugh and do 'em reason,
> Least those who dont, should be brought in for Treason.
> Well, Faith and Troth thou art a happy Dog,
> And can'st design and flatter, fawn and Cog,
> With a whole Audience, banter'd by an Epilogue,
> When next thou dost employ thy working Brains,
> Take modestly thy Fate, Husband thy Gains,
> And learn to speak with Reverence of *James*.

Mountfort's comment on these allegations is brief: "*I dont know that I meddle with any State Affairs in my Play; and for* Satyr, *I'll swear he has found out what I never meant.*" Another effusion in couplets hailing the author of *The Successful Strangers* ironically as "the Shaksphear of our present age" caused him not the slightest concern, for he was ready to assert that he does not write for fame but that all his "*Works are hab nab at a Venture.*"

Earlier in the preface from which the passages just quoted are taken, Mountfort makes some interesting remarks of a personal nature:

1. P. 27.

I have a natural Inclination to Poetry, which was born and not bred in me; I endeavour to do well, but have not Learning enough to be positive it is so; yet my Industry should not be despised, when I confess my weakness; But the Town are as unwilling to encourage a young Author, as the Play house a young Actor. . . .

I know I have a great many Enemies, but why they are so, is more than they know, I cannot remember any person I ever injur'd willingly: If my opinion be Obnoxious to some, why, that I must account for Above. And 'tis very hard I may not enjoy it here, when my side's uppermost; and yet those who are of a contrary mind, are allowed theirs quietly. I thought I had been beneath their scorn, but I find their malice excuses none.

In this particular instance industry and a *"natural Inclination to Poetry"* were rewarded. The result was a play with several capital scenes of humor and of bustling action. Its success must have convinced Mountfort, even if he had not realized it before, that it was better to woo the Muse of Comedy than to try to improve upon *The Injur'd Lovers*, and so during his leisure moments in the busy months which followed he took time to write another play in light vein with the scene laid, however, not in a foreign land, but in his own country. When *The Successful Strangers* was published, it was dedicated to Thomas Wharton, one of the most prominent of the Whigs, then a member of the Privy Council and comptroller of His Majesties Household, but famous also as the author of the satirical ballad "Lilliburlero," [1] which he boasted had sung a king out of three kingdoms.

A few lines only in *The Successful Strangers* might properly be criticized by an upholder of the Stuart cause. It is evident, however, that the actor had expressed him-

---

1. For the tune see William Chappell, *Old English Popular Music* (London, 1893), II, 58–60.

self in some place disrespectfully of the late king. The verses quoted above tell him to "learn to speak with Reverence of *James.*" Tom Brown was later to designate Mountfort "a base and unmannerly *Whig,*" who did "banter the lawful King of this great Nation" and called "*God's Anointed* a foolish old Prig." [1] Langbaine may be referring to such an utterance when, in his account of Mountfort, he remarks, "I have seen some Copies of Verses in Manuscript writ by our Author, but not being in print, that I know of, I forbear to mention them." [2]

The verses in question are probably those with the title "*CURSE*, 1690. by Mr. Munfort," which were later to appear in a volume of poems on state affairs: [3]

> Curs'd be the Stars which did Ordain
> Queen *Bess* a Maiden-Life should Reign;
> Married she might have brought an Heir,
> Nor had we known a *S——t* here.
> Curs'd be the Tribe who at *White-Hall*
> Slew one o' th' Name, and slew not all.
> Curs'd be the Second, who took Gold
> From *France*, and *Britain*'s Honour Sold;
> But Curs'd of all be *J——* the last,
> The worst of Kings, of Fools the best;
> And doubly Cursed be those Knaves,
> Who out of Loyalty would make us Slaves;
> Curs'd be the Clergy who desire ⎫
> The *French* to bring in *James* the Squire, ⎬
> And save your Church so as by Fire. ⎭
>
>   Curs'd be the Earl of *T——ton*,
> Who almost had Three Lands undone;
> Who out of Fear, of Pride, or Gain,
> Betray'd our Land, and lost her Main.

---

1. See p. 161.
2. P. 379.
3. *A New Collection of Poems Relating to State Affairs* (London, 1705), pp. 490–491.

Curs'd be the Ministers of State
Who keep our Fleet till 'tis too late;
Who have Six Weeks the Cause disputed,
When the whole in Two might have Recruited.
Curs'd be the Name of *English-man*,
To Curse it more live *T——ton*.
Let Resolution only be
King *William*'s Noble Property:
He hath done what we ne'er could do, ⎫
Ill to himself, to us been true, ⎬
Prove that among us and curse me too. ⎭

The poem could not have been completed in its present form before the middle of August, 1690, — that is, six months after February 10, the date of the publication of *The Successful Strangers*.[1] The latter portion not only contemns Arthur Herbert, Earl of Torrington, who had refused to engage the French fleet off Beachy Head on June 30, but also expresses disgust for the dilatory tactics of the ministers of state. There is no reason why the first fifteen lines, which are directed against the Stuarts and their adherents, may not have been in circulation during the first month of the year. If so, they might have come to the attention of the person who advised Mountfort to speak with reverence of James.

X

Within a short time of the performance of his fellow-actor's tragi-comedy, George Powell, who with Mountfort had been one of the two successful strangers, was to venture his first play, *The Treacherous Brothers*. Although a few years before it had been difficult for a new work to gain admittance to the theatre, it was, Powell says in his preface, "*Justice you shou'd have as great a glut of [new*

1. *The London Gazette*, No. 2529 (February 3–6, 1689/90).

plays] *now: for this reason, this little Prig makes bold to
thrust in with the Crowd.*" Some of the more experienced
dramatists began to rail at the injustice of the company
"*in indulging such inconsiderable Invaders of their Province,
the Stage*"; but, Powell continues, "*considering that greater
Bodies move slow, and the other weightier, massier Sense,
now in Rehearsal, and Study, cou'd not so easily be hammer'd
into the Players Heads, nor got up fast enough; I resolv'd the
Town shou'd not be so disoblig'd, as to have a whole* Hillary-
Term *with never a new* Play; *and so I understudy'd, and
jirckt up my little* Whipster: *This lighter toy, like a Dance
between the Acts, in pure Complausance.*"

The Hilary-term whipster was helped on its way by
Mountfort, who wrote both prologue and epilogue. The
former, which was spoken by Mrs. Knight, begins:

> *New Plays is still the Cry of the whole Town,*
> *Therefore to day, young* Powell *gives you one;*
> *The fellow never writ before this time,*
> *And I am come to plead his Cause in Rhime;*
> *You may be sure that writing is grown scarce,*
> *When he sets up for Prose, and I for Verse;*
> *Variety of Plays, like Women, all*
> *Desire, and both, when had, grow dull.*

After some lines on the uncertainty of plays and women,
it returns once more to the author:

> *Our Scribler don't at all you sharp Wits dread,*
> *He writes as Bullies fight, not for Renown, but Bread;*
> *I've heard there goes a curse with Poetry,*
> *Which many Authors know, call'd Poverty.*
> *But as for Players,*
> *They can no greater curse then being Players deserve,*
> *For write or not write, we are sure to starve;*
> *You all are leaving us to serve the Nation,*
> *Our men and we shall have a long Vacation.*

The prologue ends with the question of what the women will do when all the men have left for the wars. The epilogue, which was delivered by Mrs. Butler in male attire, contains the conventional plea not to damn the play:

> *See't but three days, and fill the House the last,*
> *He shall not trouble you again in haste.*

This supplication was not in vain, and on the third day these words appeared in the epilogue:

> *He thanks the goodness of his this days Friends,*
> *You've fill'd the House, and he has gain'd his ends.*

The tragedy was, in the main, acted by younger members of the company. Betterton, Kynaston, Sandford, and Mrs. Barry were absent from the cast, as well as the three principal comedians. Williams played Ithocles, the lover of the Queen's niece Marcelia, acted by Mrs. Bracegirdle. The Queen's brother Meleander gave Alexander [1] a longer rôle than any he had performed heretofore. Mrs. Butler once more donned the clothes of a boy as Statilia, who under the name of Lattinius follows Meleander and is finally rewarded by marrying him. Mrs. Boutell again acted the part of a queen as Semanthe, and her confidante Armena, who behaves treacherously, was taken by Mrs. Jordan. The play, however, largely rests upon the shoulders of the actors who appear as the King of Cyprus and the treacherous brothers, Menaphon and Orgillus. They were respectively the author, Mountfort, and John Hodgson, a recent acquisition to the troupe.

The plot is somewhat reminiscent of *Othello*, although the details are different. Until almost the end, Menaphon, a villain of the deepest dye, who is given to soliloquy, is

---

1. Alexander is usually identified with John Verbruggen.

master of the situation. Because he has been repulsed by the Queen, to whom he makes love, he would be revenged by having the King feel tortures great as his. Orgillus also has a grievance and is therefore ready to join him in his plans. Menaphon is able to instil the poison of jealousy into his royal master and promises to show him the Queen and Ithocles in the act of sin. With the assistance of Armena, the two victims are drugged and placed together on a couch. The King is furious and orders them to be put to death, but Menaphon, in order to divert suspicion, begs him on his knees to spare her time for repentance. When later he learns that the King is about to weaken, he hints at the dishonor that has been brought upon him by his wife, and the ruler is once more hardened. Fearing that Armena may betray her part in the stratagem, he persuades Orgillus to poison her; afterwards the brother feels remorse and is ready to confess the truth. Menaphon stabs him, but death is delayed until he has been brought to the King and told his story. The victims are of course released, and Menaphon, who remains a monster to the last, regrets that his purpose has been thwarted. If the Queen had ended her hated life, he opines, he would have borne the hottest plagues of hell,

> Rattled the Chains of my Infernal Goal,
> As Peals of Joy that I had left thee here,
> With greater torments than I felt below.
>   Have smil'd to think on thy distracted Soul,
>   And laught when all the damn'd besides did howl.

This is his exit speech, but the audience was later allowed to see him well punished for his crimes. A stage direction reads: "*The Scene drawn discovers* Men[aphon] *Executed, being flung from a* Battlement *upon Spikes.*"

The Machiavellian villain was not a type that Mountfort was often called upon to play. The beau and the witty young man of the world were the parts in which he was most pleasing, and such rôles he acted at Whitehall in 1690, the only year during the reign of William and Mary that plays were given at court on the birthdays of the king and the queen. From a few entries in the warrant books of the lord chamberlain [1] we learn something about the preparations. On April 28 Dorset directed Sir Christopher Wren "to cause the Theatre in Whitehall to bee made ready for a play to bee acted there upon Wednesday night next the 30 of this moneth being the Queenes birthday"; on April 29 he informed the Earl of Devonshire of "His Maties pleasure that the same proportion of fireing, Bread and Wine be delivered for the use of His Maties Comoedians every night they Act at Court as hath been accustomed"; and on April 30 he sent an order to Daniel Child, keeper of His Majesty's Standing Wardrobe in Whitehall, requiring him "to lend a large Lookeing glasse for the play of Sr Courtly Nice which is to be Acted before Theire Maties this Evening and after that Service done to be returned to you againe." *Sir Courtly* without Mountfort would in 1690 have been like *Hamlet* without Betterton.

Apparently the young actor acquitted himself with such distinction that when it was decided to give a performance at court on the king's birthday, the play chosen was once more a comedy in which he carried the principal part. On October 28 [2] the Earl of Montagu, master of the Great Wardrobe, received a notification signifying that it was

1. L.C. 5/150, pp. 72, 73, 74. The last entry is noted by Nicoll, p. 319. See also Miss Boswell, p. 292.
    2. L.C. 5/150, p. 164 (Miss Boswell, pp. 144-145).

His Majesty's pleasure that he provide and deliver a new
"Curtaine for the Theatre in Whitehall of the Same Stuffe
& of the Same Colours as the Old curtaine onely one of
the Colours to be Orange the Same to be made ready to
be put vp on the fourth of November next being his
Ma^ts Birthday and that it be made to draw vp & lett
downe as the other." Luttrell informs us that the day was
observed "very strictly, by shutting up the shops, firing
the great guns at the Tower, ringing of bells, and bonefires
at night; their majesties dined publickly at Whitehall,
where was a great resort of nobility and gentry, and at
night was a consort of musick, and a play afterwards." [1]
When the orange curtain was drawn, the audience was
entertained by Mrs. Behn's salacious but animated comedy, *The Rover*. How Mountfort played Willmore is told
by Colley Cibber:

The *agreeable* was so natural to him, that even in that dissolute
Character of the *Rover* he seem'd to wash off the Guilt from Vice,
and gave it Charms and Merit. For tho' it may be a Reproach
to the Poet to draw such Characters not only unpunish'd but rewarded, the Actor may still be allow'd his due Praise in his excellent Performance. And this is a Distinction which, when this
Comedy was acted at *Whitehall*, King *William*'s Queen *Mary*
was pleas'd to make in favour of *Monfort*, notwithstanding her
Disapprobation of the Play.

Mrs. Behn's work, which had been originally presented
as early as March, 1677, by the old Duke's Company, had
been a favorite with royalty. It was seen by King Charles
on January 22, 1685, and it had been given at Whitehall
before King James on October 29, 1685, and again on January 19, 1687.[2] "Dear mad *Willmore*" had in the first

1. *A Brief Historical Relation* (Oxford, 1857), II, 125.
2. L.C. 5/147, pp. 68, 361 (Nicoll, pp. 312, 313).

instance been taken by Smith, and he may have kept the rôle until his withdrawal from acting, which took place not long after May, 1687. Probably Mountfort had had possession of the part for at least two and a half or three years. There is no record of the other actors who appeared in this birthday performance. It is not unlikely that Betterton and Underhill continued playing their original rôles of Colonel Belvile and Ned Blunt; but whether Mrs. Betterton, who now acted but infrequently and then usually in matronly rôles in tragedies, again attempted the youthful Florinda is a question. One cannot help wondering also whether Mrs. Barry may not have, for the occasion, relinquished Hellena to Mrs. Mountfort.[1] This bold young lady, although designed for a nun, is poorly fitted for the cloistered life and is ready to find some mad companion. Masquerading as a gipsy and later as a boy, she has many a merry encounter with the rover until finally they agree to wed. Willmore and Hellena seem made for the pair who had played Young Wealthy and Maria, Antonio and Morayma.

In addition to these two special performances at court, the queen had in that year seen five other plays, in two of which — *The Rival Queens* and *The Successful Strangers* — Mountfort had undoubtedly appeared. Whether he acted in the operas *Circe* and *The Prophetess* is not known, but Cibber's words concerning his ability as a singer should not be forgotten. His name is not given opposite a part in the original cast of *Amphytrion*.

When the latter work was presented in the autumn of 1690, Thomas Southerne was ready with *Sir Anthony Love,*

---

1. On February 18, 1703, Mrs. Verbruggen (formerly Mrs. Mountfort) played Hellena to the Willmore of Wilks.

a comedy in which Mountfort was given the principal male rôle, but which in reality was a vehicle for his wife. Here she again donned breeches and swaggered impudently as a young man. So pleased was the author with her acting that in his dedication of the printed play to Sir Thomas Shipwith he wrote enthusiastically:

You know the Original of Sir Anthony, and therefore can best judge, how the Copy is drawn; tho' it won't be to my advantage to have 'em too narrowly compar'd; her Wit is indeed inimitable, not to be painted: Yet I must say, there's something in my Draught of her, that carries a resemblance, and makes up a very tolerable Figure: And since I have this occasion of mentioning Mrs. Montford, I am pleased, by way of Thanks, to do her that publick Justice in Print, which some of the best Judges of these Performances, have, in her Praise, already done her, in publick places; that they never saw any part more masterly play'd: and as I made every Line for her, she has mended every Word for me; and by a Gaiety and Air, particular to her Action, turn'd every thing into the Genius of the Character.

Sir Anthony Love became a popular success, especially with the women who flocked to the theatre on the third and sixth days, the author's benefit performances. As Lucy, Sir Gentle Golding's former mistress, who now wears male attire and goes by the name of Sir Anthony Love, Mrs. Mountfort had a part which held the center of the stage so completely that the other characters seem insignificant in comparison. The scene is laid in Montpelier, to which place Lucy has followed her lover Valentine, played by Mountfort. He does not recognize her, and there falls in love with Floriante (Mrs. Butler). When the two are prevented from eloping, Sir Anthony would lighten Valentine's disappointment by having him conducted to another person. This proves to be herself in woman's clothes;

she insists that he marry his French love, for the latter will be less dangerous as a wife than as a mistress, and later she makes the wedding possible by shifting garments with Floriante. As Sir Anthony, she causes Ilford (Williams) many jealous moments when she wins the interest of Volante (Mrs. Knight). After the affair has gone so far that marriage seems inevitable, she has Ilford play the priest and then turns the "wife" over to the lover. She also tries to provoke the jealous and cowardly Count Verole (Sandford) into fighting; and, after plying Palmer, the cheating pilgrim (Powell), with drugged wine, she takes his casket from him. Dressed as Floriante, she in the end marries Sir Gentle Golding (Bowen), but when he discovers who she really is, he is willing to pay any sum to be rid of her.

Hodgson and Mrs. Bracegirdle, who spoke the prologue, had but little to do as Count Canaile and his daughter Charlott. Of the players carrying lesser parts, it should be mentioned that Colley Cibber in this comedy acted his first recorded rôle. Little did his colleagues in *Sir Anthony Love* realize that the youth of nineteen who spoke the few lines allotted to Sir Gentle's servant would nearly fifty years later write the book that would chiefly keep their memories alive.

XI

The season of 1690–1691 was the busiest of Mountfort's career. Not only did he act nine new rôles, eight of which were the leading male parts, but he also prepared a comedy of his own and assisted in the writing or presentation of three other plays. The most important of the three was *Distress'd Innocence*, the best of the works of Elkanah

Settle, the Whig poet, who before he turned Tory had had his name coupled by Dryden with Shadwell's in eternal ridicule. This tragedy was approved by the audience, and, when compared with such fare as *The Injur'd Lovers* and *The Treacherous Brothers*, it amply deserved to be. In the dedication, Settle, after expressing his pleasure with the company for "dressing [his] Play to so much Advantage," continued:

But above all I must make my publick Acknowledgements to Mr. *Betterton* for his several extraordinary Hints to the height-ning of my best Characters, nor am I a little indebted to Mr. *Montfort*, for the Last Scene of my Play which he was so kind to write for me.

In addition to contriving the final episode, Mountfort acted the principal part of the Christian general Hormidas. Through the plots of Otrantes, the general of the Persian forces whom he had supplanted, the King is turned against him, recalls him from his campaign, and is made to believe that he instigated the burning of the Temple of the Sun. Hormidas is then deprived of his command and given the lowly task of watering the camels. But he bears his mis-fortunes with patience. For a brief moment he is con-vinced that his wife has become untrue to him with Otrantes, who has been elevated to his post; but when he learns that she had been drugged and is thus an innocent victim, he begs her to forgive him his accusations. They lament that they must never return to each other's arms; instead they must in cloisters prepare for their newer spousals in heaven. The passages which Mrs. Brace-girdle, who acted the devoted wife Cleomira, shared with Mountfort are truly pathetic and have a restraint that contrasts favorably with the wild words of the author's earlier *The Empress of Morocco*.

The other important parts were well wrought and, judging from the names of the players, were probably well taken. Isdigerdes, the misguided Persian king who falls a prey to the machinations of the villain, was acted by Bowman. The treacherous Otrantes and his abettor in crime, Rugildas, tested the abilities of Kynaston and Sandford. The proud Orundana who believes herself to be the King's daughter and who commits suicide upon learning that she is not the heiress to the throne was suited to Mrs. Barry; and the captive prince Theodosius, who loves her for herself and not for any title, went to Powell. Hodgson had the short but far from thankless rôle of the Christian bishop Audas, who is put to death, having been falsely accused of burning the temple, and whose speech made before he is led forth to execution is the most eloquent in the play.[1]

The task of writing the final scene for another person's tragedy is not an enviable one. It was apparently decided that *Distress'd Innocence* should end with plenty of action and many deaths. Mountfort begins with Rugildas "*dragging in* Cleomira *with a Dagger in his Hand*" and threatening to kill her. A clashing of swords is heard, and Hormidas enters, telling his followers to remain behind, for he would have revenge alone. Knowing that his wife will be killed if he approaches, he begs Rugildas to stay his hand and promises to plead to the King for his life, which is forfeit. But Rugildas would like to know what to do with his life if it is granted: he will live abhorred and shunned, a

---

[1]. See F. C. Brown, *Elkanah Settle, His Life and Works* (Chicago, 1910), pp. 93-95.

"Wandring Scandal through the Persian Empire," for neither man nor heaven can pardon his crimes. Cleomira then speaks and would rather have him strike than owe her life to such a barbarous monster. As the King is announced, Rugildas stabs her. Hormidas then runs at him; the two men close, and each receives his death wound from the other, as Isdigerdes enters and orders them to be parted. To his royal master's question about what could provoke him to such an action, Rugildas replies

> Revenge: I knew that I should die for them,
> And now they die with me,

but the command that he be put to torture is thwarted by death. Cleomira and Hormidas also have not long to live; but before they die, the King orders that their infant son be brought back to "his Native Nest, the Royal Cedar." The play then concludes as Isdigerdes is left alone to envy the lot of the pair "blest with Joys Divine." [1]

Mountfort's contributions to Settle's tragedy did not cease with the final speech of the King, for he wrote the epilogue, which was spoken by Mrs. Knight, and which contained a special plea for the turncoat author who in order to keep up with the political procession had been a Whig and then a Tory and was now once more a Whig:

1. Genest, II, 3, notes that the stage-effect produced at Hormidas' entrance is precisely the same as that in the last act of Robert Jephson's *Braganza* (first acted in 1775), but that the scene ends differently. In the later play, Louisa, duchess of Braganza, is threatened by Velasquez, who draws a dagger. Don Juan, the duke, enters and is told not to approach,
> "Or, by the blackest furies hell ere loos'd,
> This dagger drinks her blood."
The duchess is defiant. Velasquez demands that the duke restore to Spain what the rebels have seized and that he be given safe conduct back to the palace; otherwise not heaven itself can save her. At that moment, Ramirez, whom he thought dead, is brought in wounded with a roll telling of all Velasquez' villainies. He is at once seized, and the duke and duchess run to each other's arms.

In vain the hopes of pleasing you we cherish,
You hate the Author, and the Play must perish.
If so, my Masters, 'tis a little hard,
Has he so Sinn'd, that he's all Mercy barr'd?
He has chang'd Sides, 'tis true, but Sirs, I pray,
Is he the only Scribbler went Astray?

Mountfort's next bit of assistance was not for an experienced playwright, but for a very minor actor, who showed himself to be a very minor dramatist in *The Mistakes, Or The False Report*. In the epilogue written by Nahum Tate the audience was told by Mrs. Butler, dressed in man's clothes, that the author Joseph Harris justifies

his Cause — for Life,
For Fame, for Liberty, for Bratts, and Wife:
He writes, but 'tis not for the sake of Writing;

and that "*Meer want our Youngsters to write Plays impowers.*" The author, who refers properly to the "many errors of this indigested trifle" and also to "the confusion and uncertainty [that] attended it, both at it's conception, and birth," says in his preface:

I might here (as it is very very Customary) beg leave to tell the World the many inconveniences this hasty Peice has been expos'd to; as the Season of the being so near *Christmas* &c. and charge all it's failings upon them; but I am sufficiently satisfyed with it's reception: and what other casualties have obstructed it's wellcome, have been exceedingly made up by Mr. *Montfort, Quem semper honoratum, &c.* Twou'd be Tautology to mention his extraordinary favours, which are already sufficiently known, and need not my suffrage: but he that will scan thoroughly the Series of his goodness to me, will find an unbyass'd kindness, and generous pitty in every step. Nor shou'd I be backward in acknowledging (I dare not call it the impartiall) favours of the pardoning Audience. . . . And here's a fresh occasion for my gratitude to Mr. *Montfort*, who in the fi[f]th Act has not only corrected the tediousness by cutting out a whole Scene, but to make the Plot more clear, has put in one of his own, which heightens his own Character, and was very pleasing to the Audience.

Probably Mountfort's greatest favor to Harris was acting the part of Ricardo, described as a "Villain of the blackest dye." A self-styled "second *Machiavell*," he is lacking in brutal courage but possesses witty malice, and like Menaphon in *The Treacherous Brothers* is given to soliloquies. Loving the daughter of the Viceroy, Miranda, he would hinder her from marrying Alberto, and so he causes the latter to think that Antonio is his rival for her hand. Antonio, however, is a suitor for Astella, Alberto's sister. It is not necessary to follow the complicated action with its scenes of misunderstandings and Ricardo's fruitless attempts to put both Alberto and Antonio out of the way. Finally, in the last act, which Mountfort "corrected," and in which he introduced a scene of his own, Ricardo, thinking he has killed Alberto, urges his own case, but in his zeal he overreaches himself and causes the Viceroy to leave him in anger. He is troubled by a guilty conscience, and so, when Alberto appears, he mistakes him for a ghost and is frightened. Kneeling, he offers to yield his title to Miranda; but after he discovers that Alberto is alive, he pretends to be penitent, begs pardon for his crimes, and then makes a final vain attempt to murder the successful lover. Experiencing a real reversal of feeling, he later acknowledges that he has been a fool to bar the love ordained by heaven. After he has been restrained from committing suicide, he begs to be killed, lest he work more mischief. Instead of being put to death, he is banished, and at the end he leaves with the intention of retreating to some lonely isle, where he will try to atone for his deeds with penitential tears.

The acting of this absurd tragi-comedy, like that of *The Treacherous Brothers*, was mainly in the hands of the younger members of the company. Mrs. Bracegirdle as the bewildered Miranda was required to shed many tears and to take a draught which proves not to be poison. Hodgson was the Viceroy Don Juan de Mendoza, who during the greater part of the action is a mere puppet in the hands of Ricardo. The mistaken young gentlemen Alberto and Antonio were played by Powell and Alexander, and the semi-comic servant Lopez, who dresses like his master, was taken by Bowen. Mrs. Butler was again forced to wear breeches and to present once more the threadbare stage-device of serving the man she loves as a page. In short, *The Mistakes* seems no more than a medium for enabling some of the junior actors to assist one of their number.

Such a statement may not be made of *King Edward the Third, With the Fall of Mortimer, Earl of March*, which had in its cast — in addition to Powell, Mountfort, Hodgson, and Mrs. Bracegirdle — such veterans as Kynaston, Sandford, Leigh, Nokes, and Mrs. Barry. Attributed to a surgeon who occasionally dabbled in the drama, John Bancroft,[1] this play was a present to Mountfort and thus any

---

1. The name of the author does not appear upon the title-page. *The Gentleman's Journal* of October, 1692, describes *Henry II* as a "new Play, by the Author of that call'd *Edward the Third.*" Gildon, p. 5, attributes *Henry II* to Bancroft, as does the author of the preface to the 1720 edition of Mountfort's plays. *Edward III* appears among plays of unknown authorship in Gildon, p. 159, and in the "List of all the English Dramatic Poets" printed with Thomas Whincop's *Scanderbeg* (London, 1747). It is attributed to Mountfort in [W. R. Chetwood], *The British Theatre* (London, 1752), p. 112. David E. Baker in *The Companion*

profits from the third day, dedication, or sale were to accrue to the actor rather than the author. It was seen by the queen and the maids of honor on February 4, 1691, and on the following October 10 the lord chamberlain ordered that there should be "payd unto William Monfort ye Sum of Tenn pounds for ye play Call'd Edward ye third acted before Her Matie the Sd Sum being assigned by ye Comedians to be received by him." [1]

It was not customary for historical plays in the late seventeenth century to omit references which might be applicable to the contemporary situation, and the present work appears to have had as one of its purposes a foreshadowing of the evils which might have beset the nation had James continued to reign and had his misgovernment not been brought to an end by the coming of William of Orange. At times one thinks that *Edward III* may have been written as an attempt to silence criticism of the present king. In the prologue occur these significant lines:

> *Here* English-Men *with pleasure may behold,*
> *How much their Liberties were priz'd of old.*
> *How hard this Prince for's Countrys freedom strove,*
> *And how both Prosper'd in each others Love.*

And in the dedication to Henry Sydney, Viscount Sydney of Sheppey, who had been one of the leaders in the movement that brought William to England, Mountfort mentions the story of the play as one dealing with the few good men about the king,

---

to the Play-House (London, 1764) avers that "*Coxeter* . . . attributes it to *John Bancroft,* who, as he says, made a Present of it to *Mountfort* the Actor." In the 1782 edition of *Biographia Dramatica* and also in the 1812 edition, the statement concerning Coxeter's attribution of the work is repeated.

1. L.C. 5/151, p. 369, 5/150, p. 306 (Nicoll, pp. 314, 319).

who with great difficulty preserv'd this Prince from the evill Machinations of *Mortimer* and his Faction, from the Potent Enemies of an Interested State; and the unnatural Connivance of a Mother (who design'd as much to usurp his Right as she really did destroy his Fathers) and the delivering their Country from the Tyranny and Oppression it had been long afflicted with, and which in all probability threatned the totall overthrow of the Establish'd Liberties of the Subject.

The scene of the play, which is a medley of fact and fiction, is laid in Nottingham, and the plot relates events in the early part of the reign. The rulers of England are Isabella, the queen mother, and her paramour, the powerful and ambitious Mortimer, but the rights of the young King are upheld by a group of nobles. Among these is Lord Mountacute, who unknown to himself is loved by Maria, the niece of Serjeant Eitherside. The latter would use her as an aid to preferment, and so he introduces her to the tool of Mortimer, the lecherous Chancellor Tarleton, who has persuaded the Queen that she may dispense with laws. A paper containing the names of those he desires to put to death, among them Mountacute, is taken by Mortimer to Tarleton and found by Maria, who carries it to Mountacute. He now learns of her tender feelings towards him, and before the interview is over, he himself is in love.

Angered with the peers because of their influence with the King, Isabella demands admittance to the council. Here she is treated coolly. After telling her that he is of age to govern and that he has chosen these men as his guides, Edward is touched by her tears at his ingratitude. The councilors, who fear he may weaken, force him away as she pleads for him to listen. In her anger at this treatment, she signs an order for the King's confinement presented to her by Mortimer. This is sent to Tarleton, who, thinking it is the commission to take the lives of Mountacute and the others, tells Maria to deliver it to Eitherside, who is to be the prosecutor; but she gives it to Mountacute, who hands it to the King. Edward and his followers then enter the castle by a secret passage and come upon Isabella and her lover. The King acts with decision by ordering Mortimer to be thrown into a dungeon, his mother to be removed, and the chancellor to be put to death. He rewards Mountacute by making him Earl of Salisbury and by giving him Maria, whom he invests with Tarleton's estate. At her plea, he spares Eitherside; and the play concludes as he is ready to lead an army to Scotland and then to France.

Mountfort's rôle was that of Lord Mountacute, the "Soul of Honour new reviv'd," the nobleman who is ready to banish sleep and pleasure until he has found a way to set the country free. Possessed of a hot temper, he has to be restrained by Sir Thomas Delamore when he has an altercation with Mortimer. Maria, the maiden who awakens his love, was acted by Mrs. Bracegirdle. The longest part, Mortimer, was taken by Williams, and the youthful King was played by Powell. Mrs. Barry portrayed Isabella, the queen mother, who loses all sense of values in her passion for Mortimer. Remorseful at the end, for her love tempted him to be ambitious, she begs that his life may be spared, but after her entreaties have been denied she leaves her son with a mother's curse upon his head. Comic parts and scenes in prose were provided for Leigh and Nokes — the former as the corrupt Tarleton, who is willing both to give and to receive bribes; the latter as the ponderous Serjeant Eitherside.

There is no contemporary statement to the effect that Mountfort had anything to do with the writing of this play. In the dedication he calls it "a Present to me," and the epilogue makes evident that

> *. . . since the Author who did this Prepare*
> *Only expects your Liking for his share,*
> *Do not Withdraw the Profit from the Player.*

The publishers of the 1720 edition of his works — in which were printed *Edward III* and *Henry II* along with four pieces by Mountfort — assert that the two historical plays *"which tho' not wholly composed by him, it is presum'd he had, at least, a Share in fitting . . . for the Stage, otherwise it cannot be supposed he would have taken the Liberty of Writing Dedications to them."* This presumption based merely on the ground that he wrote the dedications seems unwarranted. However, the facts that *Edward III* was a present to him and that he was therefore entitled to the receipts on the third day indicate that he doubtless scanned the script with a critical eye and made such changes as would seem necessary to an experienced man of the theatre.

XII

About a year after his first attempt at playwriting, *The Treacherous Brothers*, the actor and self-styled "*Mushroom Scribler*" George Powell again begged the indulgence of the audience for a tragedy. Fortified with a prologue by Haynes, an epilogue by D'Urfey, and a cast chosen from the younger members of the company, *Alphonso, King of Naples*, was launched. Powell's second work was described as having

some Wit, tho' mix'd with many a Fau't,
Some little Fancy too; but as for Plot,
There are so many New ones found elsewhere,
He thought not worth his time to make one here. [1]

The statement contains the truth so far as the plot is concerned. Once more we have the story of the general against whom the ruler is prejudiced; the ruler's stubbornly favoring the suit of another person for the hand of his daughter; and the resulting deaths of all concerned except the ruler, who lives on to realize that he is responsible for the trouble. The king whose name gives the title to the play was taken by Bowman, who had a short time before acted a similar part as Isdigerdes in *Distress'd Innocence*. The author did not as in his earlier tragedy keep the longest rôle for himself, but here played Ferdinand, the prince of Thessaly who is a suitor for the hand of Urania. He is jealous and plants the seeds of fear for the general's ambition in the mind of Alphonso. It is he who takes the general prisoner and then later by one of those unexpected and unaccountable acts found only in the theatre becomes so impressed by the brave spirit of his rival that he declares he is vanquished and bids him come to his arms. After embracing, the two then fight for their love, and each is mortally wounded in the combat.

The lovers, Cesario the general and Urania the princess, were, as in *Distress'd Innocence*, played by Mountfort and Mrs. Bracegirdle. Here once more they acted scenes of pleading, defiance, farewell, and death. They first appear together outside the city as she, veiled, comes to Cesario and tells how her father intends banishing him unless he

1. Epilogue written by Tom D'Urfey.

gives free consent to her marriage with Ferdinand. After his suit has been scorned by the King, the two decide to go to the Arcadian plain and there live a pastoral life. Although they are molested by bandits en route, their journey ends fortunately when they meet Cesario's banished brother Tachmas and are taken to the cell where he lives as a hermit. Here they are discovered by Ferdinand and haled back to Naples. Alphonso now determines that Cesario shall be put to death and that Urania shall marry the prince of Thessaly. But Urania is defiant, and her father, after ordering that she be confined to her chamber and that Cesario be sent to prison, leaves in a rage. The lovers then bid each other farewell and part. They are together once more in the concluding scene. As Cesario and Ferdinand lie dying, Urania is led in bleeding, having stabbed herself, and gives up the ghost, "a Virgin in [her] Husbands Arms."

During the busy season of 1690–1691 Mountfort did not devote all his energies to rehearsing the woes of unhappy lovers, but he returned more than once to rôles of the young man about town, reckless in action, but good at heart. Such a part was that of Sir William Rant, the hero of *The Scowrers*, a comedy by the poet-laureate, who had provided well for Mountfort in the younger Belfond and Wildish. Sir William Rant has gained notoriety as a scourer, or person who in the mid-hours of the night delights in fighting the watch, breaking windows, and smashing the interiors of taverns. So great is the fame of his exploits that others are desirous of emulating him; but, after meeting Eugenia, he is ready to be as remarkable in penitence as he ever was in wickedness. He gaily pursues her and, before the end of the play, causes her mother

Lady Maggot, who has an utter hatred of him, many uncomfortable moments. Playing opposite Mountfort as Eugenia, who finds in Sir William Rant the prettiest man her eyes ever beheld, and who rebels against her mother's authority, was not the actor's wife, as might have been expected, but Mrs. Barry. This character is presented as wittier and livelier than her sister Clara, who is called "Mrs. Milksop" by Lady Maggot and who was acted by Mrs. Bracegirdle. These two young women will not consent to wed until their lovers show that they are truly repentant by serving as probationers for one year. Sir William's comrade in dissipation, Wildfire, who is drawn to Clara, and who is pursued by Lady Maggot, was played by Williams; and the father, Mr. Rant, who delivers a moralistic lecture in blank verse, was presumably wellfitted for Kynaston.

As usual Shadwell was ready with several humorous parts. The aged scourer Tope, who has outdrunk two generations, and who laughs at the idea of going to bed sober, was a good rôle for Leigh; and Bowman, who was called upon to act the brainless beau as well as the stern ruler, was here cast as the city-wit Whachum, whose greatest ambition is to scour in the manner of Sir William. His uncle, Sir Humphrey Maggot, the alderman with Jacobite leanings and a fondness for news-letters, was played by George Bright; and Mrs. Leigh took the part of his domineering wife with an ungovernable temper. Less important was Mrs. Corey's rôle — that of the governess Priscilla, who is more than once the victim of Lady Maggot's fury, and who is made drunk by Sir William's valet. Inferior as the comedy is to *The Squire of Alsatia* or *Bury Fair*, it did contain several good acting parts, and in its far from savage satire of scouring it treated an abuse which was a real menace to the contemporary Londoner.

Although there was not a little of the sentimental in the character taken by Mountfort in *The Scowrers*, the same remark may not be made of his part in *Love for Money: or, The Boarding School*.[1] Jack Amorous, in D'Urfey's comedy, is described by the author as "a witty Extravagant of the Town, generous and well natur'd." He persists in adoring women, although they have been the utter ruin of his fortunes; and, despite the warning of his friend Merriton, he refuses to believe that his mistress Betty Jiltall is false to him. Dressing her in East Indian attire, he would have his grasping uncle, Sir Rowland Rakehell, believe that she is the heiress whom he has defrauded of her estate. So pleased is Amorous with her acting of the part that he promises to marry her instantly if his uncle will settle one thousand pounds a year upon him. Then he learns from the Frenchman Le Prate of her falsehood. Now he realizes that he loved her beyond reason, and his nature is shocked "to think such barbarous Ingratitude could injure such true Love." He gains revenge by getting back his former settlement of three hundred pounds a year. Thinking that she is now without means of support, he is surprised and angered later to find her richly dressed and the wife of his uncle. He exposes her for what she is, and at the end, although he cannot marry the real heiress

1. See Robert S. Forsythe, *A Study of the Plays of Thomas D'Urfey* (Cleveland, 1916), pp. 67–74; also Kathleen M. Lynch, "Thomas D'Urfey's Contribution to Sentimental Comedy" in *Philological Quarterly*, IX (1930), 249–259. I have followed Forsythe in placing the first performances of the play in 1691. Amorous says of Betty, p. 37, "I settled an Estate upon her in 87, carried her to *Flanders* in 88, and spent two thousand pounds upon her in 89, brought her over with me in 90, and now this present year find my self jilted."

Mirtilla, he is assured that he will receive that part of his estate of which his uncle has deprived him. The mistress, whose duplicity brings this easy-going youth to his senses and whose philosophy is summarized in her words, "Love for Money ever whilst you live," was acted by Mrs. Butler, who for a change now had a rôle that required no wearing of masculine attire.

The play, with Mountfort in the principal part, was an undoubted success, and D'Urfey acknowledged himself "sensibly oblig'd both to the Patentees and Sharers for dressing it so well, and to all the Actors in general for their extraordinary performance." On the first day there was some disturbance in the pit; and Gildon reports that dancing-masters and friends to boarding-schools at that time made an attempt to damn it.[1] Some persons alleged that the dramatist had lived at a boarding-school near London all the previous summer and "in return of their hospitable Civility, writ this Play ungratefully to expose 'em." When D'Urfey came to prepare his preface, he informed the town that he had never been obliged more than for common courtesies to any of the schools and that he had returned all such courtesies. He also denied that he wrote the comedy to reflect on a particular family or noble person.

Like nearly all of D'Urfey's later plays, *Love for Money* is cluttered with characters and contains many strands of plot. The two serious parts, which savor of the sentimental, Young Merriton and Mirtilla, were played by Hodgson and Mrs. Bracegirdle. Described as a "great lover of Learning, and skill'd in Philosophy, Poetry, and Musick," Merriton falls in love with a girl at the boarding-school,

1. P. 51.

which he visits as a dancing-master. Although she loves him, she will not consent to a wedding because she has no money and feels that "Poverty and Marriage never suit." When she learns later that she is an heiress, she is ready to give him her fortune. Now he refuses, even though he still loves her. But after she has left, he feels that he would be a fool to lose her, and so he decides to play the game in order that she may not twit him with her benefits in the future. Needless to say, all ends well.

The novelty which D'Urfey introduced was that of placing several scenes at a boarding-school in Chelsea and representing certain of the types to be found there: Miss Jenny and Miss Molly, the awkward girls who are always eating bread and butter, played by Mrs. Knight and Mrs. Davies; the harassed teacher, Crowstitch, acted by Mrs. Corey; and the two masters, who finally elope with the girls, performed by Bowman and Kirkham. Cave Underhill was the cheating uncle Sir Rowland Rakehell, who believes that "Reason and Vertue are as useless drugs as Learning and Poetry." Powell and Bright appeared as the two Braggs, son and father, the former trying to pass as a captain and the latter, a grenadier in the army of King William, forever stripping his son of his fine clothing. Bowen was the French fop Le Prate, whose blunder brings Amorous to his senses; and Leigh now wore woman's clothes as Lady Addleplot, the active opponent to the present government and the iron-handed ruler of her husband. A new actor, Thomas Doggett, made a decided impression in a comparatively minor part constructed along conventional lines — that of Deputy Nicompoop, the henpecked husband of Lady Addleplot. This is the first rôle of which we have record acted at Drury Lane by

Doggett, who performed the part "inimitably" in Downes' words, and who was soon, upon the retirement of Nokes, to take his place as one of the principal low comedians.

After the Jacobite uprising comes to naught, Mirtilla and Young Merriton are ready to wed, Rakehell and Betty Jiltall are thwarted, and Jack Amorous learns that he will receive that part of his estate which his uncle had kept from him by unjust means, the performance of *Love for Money* was brought to a close by a rather coarse epilogue spoken by Mountfort and Mrs. Butler. The two players talk about their parts; they point out the cuckolds in the upper row — "*Rich Goldsmiths, Mercers, Taylors, Brewers, Bakers*" — and they note the cuckold-makers in the pit.

Butl.   *Well, these abusive Jests will never do,*
         The Audience hates 'em;
Moun. *That's a sign they're true.*
Butl.   *'Dslife 'tis enough to cry the Playhouse down,*
         Lee's part and mine abuses half the Town.
Moun. *Good Satyr's no abuse.*
Butl.   *Not where the lash is felt?*
         Faith Monford *thour't a Coxcomb.*
Moun. *You're a Jilt.*
Butl.   *Made so here, only by a Poet's pen;*
         Send him his part, I'll never play't agen.
                     [Throws away the part, and *Exit.*

Mountford *to the Audience.*
         This is a Trick, and done, or Im a Chouse,
         To get a greater pension from the House;
         I therefore, on the Author's part appear
         To beg excuse for th' Entertainment here:
         And now I from my Wife *some time can borrow,*
         I'll swinge her — but I'll make her play't to morrow.

After several performances of *Love for Money*, the company was ready for another production, and again Mount-

fort was cast for the leading rôle. The play was once more
the work of D'Urfey, an adaptation of *Bussy D'Ambois*.
The reviser, who had seen Hart act Bussy, felt that Chapman's tragedy, despite its "obsolete Phrases and intoler-
able Fustian," contained some extraordinary beauties, and
so he was ready to make his version. He then tried to
get it acted, but in vain, until Mountfort — in D'Urfey's
words — "did me the Favour; who, though he was mod-
estly very diffident of his own Action, coming after so great
a Man as Mr. *Hart*, yet had that Applause from the Audience, which declared their Satisfaction, and with which I
am sure he ought to be very well contented."

Once again Mountfort succeeded in a rôle in which Hart
had won renown. A very different part from Alexander the
Great, Bussy, even in D'Urfey's inferior version, contained
much that would commend itself to the actor: the poverty-
stricken gentleman who through a gift from Monsieur
rises to become a favorite of the King, but who, despite his
rich clothes, cannot play the courtier; the lover to whom
Tamira plighted her first vows; the clever duelist who
never comes off second in fair fight; the outspoken person
who gives the lie to the Duke of Guise and who spares no
words in telling Monsieur exactly what he thinks of him.
Mountfort rose to the occasion, for a pamphlet directed
againt D'Urfey and called *Wit for Money* reported, "those
that are Judges say, that were it not for Mr. *M-fords* excellent acting, which is the Soul of the Play, it would have
been still-born." [1]

The actors who assisted in the production of this "*Len-
ten Dish*" were again mainly the junior members of the
troupe. Kynaston, however, played the Duke of Guise,

1. P. 24.

who quarrels with Bussy because of his insolence, and who is later an agent of revenge; and Mrs. Corey once more acted the rôle of governess as Teresia. The other important parts were in the hands of Mrs. Bracegirdle as Tamira, Bussy's love; Hodgson as Monsieur, the King's brother; Powell as Montsurry, Tamira's husband; and Freeman as Henri III.

With such varied new rôles as the unfortunate generals Hormidas and Cesario, the Machiavellian villain Ricardo, the faithful subject Lord Mountacute, the young men about town Valentine, Sir William Rant, and Jack Amorous, and the ill-fated favorite Bussy D'Ambois, Mountfort had a very taxing season. It is pleasing to know that Alexander D'Avenant recognized that fact and did "give to Mr Mountfort 20 Guineas upon account of his extraordinary Study for the service of ye Theatres." [1] But in addition to playing these eight new parts, Mountfort also took the principal rôle in his own comedy, which was presented before the summer of 1691.

XIII

Why so many novelties were given during these months is explained by the opening words of the prologue to *Greenwich Park*: [2]

1. Deposition of Joseph Williams, dated October 22, 1691 (P.R.O. C 24, 1141/11), from a photostat — in the Theatre Collection, Harvard College Library — of a document found in the Public Record Office by Professor Leslie Hotson.

2. All quotations are from the edition with the following title-page: "Greenwich-Park: A Comedy. Acted at the Theatre-Royal, By Their Majesties Servants. Written by William Mountfort. London: Printed for J. Hindmarsh at the Golden-Ball in Cornhill, R. Bentley, in Russel-street in Covent-Garden, and A. Roper, at the Mitre in Fleet-street. And are to be sold by Randal Taylor, near Stationers-Hall. MDCXCI."

With the sad prospect of a Long Vacation,
The Fear of War, and Danger of the Nation;
Hard we have toil'd this Winter for new Plays,
That we might live in these Tumultuous Days.

For this reason and also for the fact which he states in his dedicatory epistle addressed to Algernon Capel, Earl of Essex, that "*Poetry . . . has ever been* [*his*] *Delight*," Mountfort was now ready with a comedy portraying characters from contemporary English life. Only the opening scenes are laid in London; then the locale shifts to Greenwich and the nearby Deptford Wells.

The plot has to do with the adventures of the two Revellers — father and son. Sir Thomas, who prides himself on the leer in his left eye, prefers carousing at Greenwich Park with the citizens Raison, a henpecked grocer, and Sasaphras, a druggist, to hanging about the court. He is very parsimonious and severe with his son, who realizes that the best way to get what he desires is to pretend that he wants just the opposite. Young Reveller is kept in pocket-money by Mrs. Raison, who has introduced him to the heiress, Florella, daughter of Lady Hazard. He loves this young lady of lively disposition and wishes to marry her. Incidentally Dorinda, who, unknown to him, is the kept mistress of his friend Lord Worthy, has seen him and fallen in love. Thus he finds himself at the center of a triangle of warring females.

After too heavy potations at a supper with Sir Thomas and his comrades, he goes to the park and there meets Dorinda. She arouses his desire; and when he responds warmly, she pretends to be angry with him for believing that she would yield upon the first conference. Becoming sobered, he begs her pardon; and she leaves with the word that he shall shortly hear from her. This interview has been observed by Mrs. Raison's maid, with the result that the mistress is soon at hand to confront her fickle lover. Reveller takes her to his lodgings, where she is compelled to hide in his bedroom at the approach of Sir Thomas and his drunken companions. The knight is suspicious, but he is prevented from forcing the door by Raison and Sasaphras.

The next day at Deptford Wells, Dorinda invites Young Reveller to dine. Florella notices the two talking and addresses him as the favorite of the whole sex. A saucy interchange of remarks ensues between the two women; then Florella unmasks and tells her much-besought lover to follow his damsel and trouble her no more. After an altercation with some beaux and bullies who become too attentive to the ladies, he goes to Dorinda.

Realizing how her lover has been straying, Florella dresses herself in boy's clothes with the intention of trying to make Mrs. Raison inconstant to him. A similar idea occurs to the grocer's wife, who also puts on male attire, hoping to draw Florella away from Reveller. The two "men" make love to Dorinda: Mrs. Raison thinking her Florella and Florella correctly believing her to be the person Reveller had conversed with earlier in the day at the Wells. Dorinda, however, is not moved by the quarreling rivals, but seizes the opportunity to box the ears of Reveller, who is talking to a strange woman. At length Florella recognizes that her opponent is Mrs. Raison in disguise, and so she plays the bully for revenge. The grocer's wife finally owns who she is, and her husband, who then appears and is also unwilling to fight, is well kicked for his cowardice.

Reveller tells Worthy of his entertainment by Dorinda, and then goes to her house, to which he is shortly afterwards followed by his friend. Here before the company he has gathered Worthy unmasks the falsehood of his mistress, and Dorinda departs in anger. But the atmosphere is soon cleared, and at the end Sir Thomas is ready to take Lady Hazard as wife; Reveller pretends that he values his freedom more than Florella and thus gets his father to insist upon their marriage; Worthy will wed Violante, Florella's sister; and Mrs. Raison gives her husband her heart.

An alert theatregoer of the spring of 1691 would probably have noticed that Mountfort's latest comedy was somewhat reminiscent of another play also by an actor that had been performed two years before, James Carlisle's *The Fortune Hunters*. Many of the characters in *Greenwich Park* correspond to similar characters in the earlier work, and the corresponding parts in each comedy were taken by the same players. Leigh as Sir William Wealthy and Sir Thomas Reveller was the brisk and coarse-grained knight who is harsh in his relations with his son. Mountfort, in the rôles of Young Wealthy and Young Reveller, played the witty and wild man about town who cuckolds a citizen and falls in love with a spirited young lady whom he finally marries. Mrs. Mountfort, as Maria and Florella, was required to engage in tilts of repartee with the young gentleman, to arouse jealousy, and to wear male attire. Nokes, who ever since acting Bisket in *Epsom Wells* was expected to play cuckolded citizens with a fondness for drinking, had such rôles in Spruce and Raison; and Mrs. Knight in both plays appeared as the faithless wife. Each comedy also had a third woman infatuated with the hero, but the Lady Sly acted by Mrs. Leigh in the earlier play is a very different person from Mrs. Barry's Dorinda, except that each is jealous.

Although these similarities exist between the two plays, the later comedy both in character and situation proceeds along very different lines. Since the audience of 1691 would find no novelty in seeing Mrs. Mountfort or Mrs. Butler wearing breeches, the thought might naturally occur to the author: Why not give Mrs. Knight, who had played opposite him in his last comedy, an opportunity to dress as a man and place her in a scene with the actress who had recently swaggered to fame as Sir Anthony Love? The result was a delightfully amusing situation. The actor who had taken leading parts in *The Squire of Alsatia*, *Bury Fair*, and *The Successful Strangers* — all plays with many good passages for Leigh, Nokes, and Underhill — would not compose a comedy without rôles for each of the matchless three, and so for Underhill was contrived the druggist Sasaphras, the companion of Sir Thomas and Raison in their carousings. The inevitable second pair of lovers, Lord Worthy and Violante, were in the hands of Hodgson and Mrs. Lassells; and the Aunt to Dorinda was a good part for Mrs. Corey. The persons who add to the movement of the scene at Deptford Wells — the knight Sir William Thoughtless, Bully Bounce, and a nameless beau — were played by Bowen, Bright, and Bowman; and Mrs. Osborn acted the minor bit of Lady Hazard.

The play, which was concluded with an epilogue spoken by Mrs. Mountfort, gave pleasure to the habitués of Drury Lane. Gildon called it "a very pretty Comedy, and has been always received with general Applause."[1] It contains many diverting scenes, such as those in which Mrs. Raison demands that her husband provide her with a coach, Sir Thomas rebukes his son, the intoxicated

1. P. 102.

Reveller confronts Dorinda in the park, Florella tilts with her lover, and the two women don breeches.[1] Mountfort provided several passages of humor of a robust quality for the comedians and also a goodly share of witty lines for himself and his wife. The principal characters are all definitely individualized. Not the least successful of these is the unfortunate Dorinda, who is swept off her feet by her passion for Reveller, becomes wildly jealous when she sees the young man's attraction for other women, forgets the claims that Worthy has upon her, and at the end departs thwarted.

The Successful Strangers and *Greenwich Park* showed that Mountfort had found himself as a dramatist. After trying tragedy, he turned to comedy and discovered that his gift lay there. His plays in this form naturally took into account his own demands as an actor and the special talents of the other members of the company. Despite the fact that *Greenwich Park* was composed for a definite group of players, it contained materials that made it a popular piece in the theatrical repertoire for nearly fifty years [2] and that even give it power to entertain in the library to-day.

XIV

So far as we may judge from the imperfect records, Mountfort was the busiest of the actors in new plays from February, 1688, to the summer of 1691. In that time he had appeared in at least eighteen new parts, all of which were long and two-thirds of which were leading rôles. In this same period, Betterton had acted in six new plays, Mrs. Barry in nine, and the principal comedian Leigh in

1. Pp. 1–3, 10–11, 23–27, 20, 52–54.   2. See Appendix B.

seventeen. During Mountfort's very active season of 1690–1691, Betterton had not appeared with him in a single new play; but in 1691–1692, as we shall now see, matters were different.

The next comedy in which Mountfort acted was presented in December, 1691, but despite the efforts of the most valued members of the company, *The Wives Excuse: or, Cuckolds Make Themselves* did not arouse the enthusiasm of the theatregoers. Southerne was unable to repeat the success of *Sir Anthony Love*, and in Dryden's words this "*Labour'd* Drama" was not

> *damn'd or hiss'd,*
> *But with a kind Civility, dismiss'd.*[1]

Although there were good judges who commended "the purity of its language,"[2] the audience was cold to a play which lacked eccentric characterization, rollicking fun, or the witty duel of the sexes.

The motif of *The Wives Excuse* is a serious one — the attempt of a woman to save her self-respect by trying to prevent her husband from appearing to be a coward and a fop. Despite his wife's protests against making his home one of the public places in town, Friendall welcomes much company. He is fond of music-meetings and of masquerades; he writes and composes; and he also finds time to carry on intrigues. Incidentally he neglects his wife. Lovemore desires to win Mrs. Friendall, and as a means to that end he wishes to discredit her husband. He therefore hires a bully to insult Friendall as the latter is returning home from a concert. Fearing that he may prove a coward, Mrs.

1. "To Mr. Southern; on his Comedy, called the Wives Excuse."
2. *The Gentleman's Journal* for January, 1691/2.

Friendall begs her husband not to draw his sword among the women. Then, not wishing him to fall into the contempt of the town, she writes a challenge which she gives to her brother to deliver, and later she tells Lovemore he may serve her by preventing the fight. A reconciliation is effected; but Lovemore gets hold of the challenge which he feels convinced is in Mrs. Friendall's handwriting. He goes to her and makes love, but she repulses him and declares that she saved her husband only to save herself. Lovemore, however, is restored to her good graces by returning the challenge, which is the only piece of evidence that can rise up against her husband.

But later, while masked, she learns from Friendall's own lips that the chief end of his marrying was to carry on his intrigues more swimmingly with the ladies, and that by passing as a very good husband he is able to grow intimate with all his wife's acquaintance. Lovemore would like to follow up this advantage; but, after asserting that he has proved his passion and tried her virtue, Mrs. Friendall begs him not to make it impossible in the future to receive him as a friend. When Friendall is finally exposed in an awkward predicament, his wife addresses him.

Mrs. Fr. Mr. *Friendall*, I'm sorry you thought it necessary to your pleasures, to make me a witness of my ill usage: you know I can, and have past many things, some Women wou'd think wrongs, as such resent 'em, and return 'em too: but you can tell how I've behav'd my self.

Mr. Fr. Like a Gentlewoman always, *M*adam, and my Wife.

Mrs. Fr. The unjust World, let what will be cause of our complaint (as there is cause sufficient still at home:) condemn us to slavery for life: And if by separation we get free, then all our Husband's faults are laid on us: This hard Condition of a Woman's fate, *I*'ve often weigh'd, therefore resolv'd to bear:

and *I* have born; O! what have *I* not born? But patience tires with such oppressing wrongs, when they come home, to triumph over me; and tell the Town how much *I* am despis'd.

Mr. Fr. I see we are both disappointed in this affair of *M*atrimony; it is not the condition you expected; nor has it the advantages *I* propos'd. Now, *M*adam, since 'tis impossible to make it happy between us, let us ev'n resolve to make it as easie as we can.

Mrs. Fr. That must be my business now.

Mr. Fr. And mine too, I assure you: look you, *M*adam, your own Relations shall provide for you at pleasure, out of my Estate; I only article that I may have a freedom of visiting you, in the round of my acquaintance.

Mrs. Fr. I must be still your Wife, and still unhappy.

The play ends with Lovemore wondering what alteration this separation must make in his fortunes, but expressing happiness that he has parted the ill-mated pair.

The parts of lover, husband, and wife were in the hands of the players who in the season of 1691–1692 became the new triad of Betterton, Mountfort, and Mrs. Barry — a worthy successor to the triad of 1682 composed of Betterton, Smith, and Mrs. Barry. Southerne, of course, could not overlook his favorite actress, who had created Sir Anthony Love, and so for Mrs. Mountfort he wrote again the longest rôle, that of the matchmaker Mrs. Wittwoud, who "has no Business Of her own, but a great deal of other Peoples" — apparently the last new part she was to act in a play with her husband. Mrs. Bracegirdle appeared as Mrs. Sightly, the young woman who is pursued by Friendall but who cares for Wellvile. The latter character, taken by Kynaston, is used as a means for Southerne to comment on his own work. Wellvile considers writing a play with the title, *The Wives Excuse: or, Cuckolds make themselves*, and in it to show a "fine young Woman marry'd to an impertinent, nonsensical, silly, entrigueing, cowardly, good-for-nothing Coxcomb" and believes, despite Friendall's insistence that the husband be made a cuckold, that he will present the wife throughout as virtuous. Mrs. Corey was once more the censorious older woman as Mrs. Teazall, who inveighs against masquerades and feels that she deserves to lose at cards for playing with company so much younger than herself.

Despite its excellence of language and serious undercurrent — possibly because of the latter — *The Wives Excuse* was treated but coldly by the patrons of Drury Lane, who were more ready to applaud its successor, *The Marriage-Hater Match'd*. Acted in January, 1692, this comedy by D'Urfey had a few mishaps at its first performance. The stage was crowded with spectators, and thus the actors were caused considerable annoyance. A faction was also on hand to give it an unwelcome reception, and the author himself was later to agree that he would never again be guilty of writing a play of such faulty length. But these shortcomings were removed by the second performance when, in the words of Charles Gildon, it "rais'd it self . . . with the general Applause of all that saw it." [1] Its right to this success, however, was challenged not long afterwards by *The Lacedemonian Mercury*, which asked the very apt question,

Whether the Town's receiving and coveting Love for Money, The Marriage Hater Match'd, *when at the same time* The Plain Dealer *and* Sir Foplin Flutter *rest untouch'd and unsought-for, be not Evidence of a very great declension in Common Sense?* [2]

1. "A Letter to Mr. D'Urfey, Occasioned by his Play Called the Marriage-Hater Match'd," printed with the play.
2. Vol. I, No. 10 (Friday, March 11, 1692).

Again Mountfort took the leading part, that of Sir Philip Freewit, the marriage-hater, and Mrs. Bracegirdle played the unfortunate Phoebe, who at the end proves his match. These two also spoke the prologue, in which the lady complains about the boy's clothes she is compelled to wear. She appears disconcerted, whereupon Mountfort exclaims:

> *A Player, and asham'd, that may be true.*
> Brace. *You think sure I'm as impudent as you.*
> Monf. *No Child; you would not do then as you do;*
> *You would not lose a Fortune for a Toy,*
> *Nor frown nor blush whene'er you Act a Boy;*
> *Or speak a* Prologue, *which you must do now,*
> *And to assist you see, I'll make your Bow.*

Then after he has bowed to the audience, she begs them to spare the poet and the play.

Although this comedy, like *Love for Money*, had too many characters and too many threads of action to make a unified effect, the principal plot, as the title suggests, has to do with the efforts of Sir Philip to escape the entanglements of matrimony. A friend who had won the woman he had once loved dies and bequeathes to him both fortune and widow. He is also pursued by a former mistress Phoebe, who wears male attire and goes by the name of Lovewell. She gets the writings and the jewels which he had locked in his closet and offers to return them on condition of marriage. After she leaves, he reflects: "My only cause of hating a Wife, is, because it is convenient for me; and Marriage in those of my humour, is just like Devotion, Lov'd and Practic'd the less, because it is Enjoyn'd us." Nettled that she has outwitted him, he would get even by having a mock-marriage performed, but the person who ties the knot proves to be a real clergyman, and the marriage-hater not too graciously accepts his fate:

> Patient, I'll Rellish pleasure dearly bought,
> And Chaw on the same Cheese, with which I'm caught.

A "very pretty Figure on the Stage" was made by Mrs. Bracegirdle as the tender Phoebe who pleads in a touching manner to her light-hearted seducer, "If I should talk t'ye of my little Boy, now, 'twould set me a crying, and you'd but laugh at me." Mrs. Barry played an opposite type in the proud and high-spirited Lady Subtle. With no respect for the memory of her husband, she is able to weep only through the aid of an onion tied in her handkerchief. She hates Sir Philip because of his intrigue with Phoebe, and is herself beset by many foolish suitors, one of whom she finally weds.

In addition to these characters concerned in the main action, D'Urfey introduced several others and thus caused Gildon in his first enthusiasm to write: "Such a variety of Humours and Characters I have seldom seen in one Play; and those so truly drawn, that they all look like principal Parts." Of these only the most important need be mentioned. Bowman again appeared as a beau, Lord Brainless, a "Pert, Noisy, Impertinent Boy," who is proud of his clothes and of his ability to make a song. Sandford acted the old-fashioned courtier Sir Lawrence Limber, who has two stupid sons and a lisping awkward daughter. The younger son Solon, dull until vexed and then "robustly stout," proved a happy rôle for Doggett, who, according to Downes, performed that part "inimitably." Leigh was the clownish Flanderkin, Myn Heer Van Grin. He is always laughing without cause until he discovers that

the widow he has married is penniless; then he is ready
to weep. Lady Bumfiddle with voice "like a Trump-
Marine" and a desire to visit wherever there is the chance
of having a good dinner was taken by Mrs. Corey. Probably the most original character in the play — that performed by Mrs. Butler — was La Pupsey, the former actress, who is never without her lap-dog Adonis, and who
delights in using hard words. Carrying the dog in masquerade costume, she spoke the epilogue.

The Marriage-Hater Match'd, with its large number of
characters, variety of action, and absurd concluding act
in which several couples are married at a masquerade,
was just the sort of comedy to appeal to an audience de-
manding mere amusement. As a work of permanent interest, it is, however, decidedly inferior to its predecessor, the
scorned *The Wives Excuse* of Southerne.

Twice more during the season of 1691–1692, Mountfort
appeared in new rôles. In each instance he played in
tragedy and acted a part second only to those performed
by Betterton and Mrs. Barry. As early as February 12,
Dryden's *Cleomenes* was reported as "intended shortly for
the Stage," [1] and it was ready for production on Saturday,
April 9, but then Queen Mary gave orders which hindered
its being acted. [2] The Earl of Rochester and others came
to the author's assistance, and the parallel which had been
pointed out was found not to be intended. Lord Chamberlain Dorset soon returned the script "*without the least
Alteration*," and within a week of its temporary ban [3]

1. *The Gentleman's Journal* for February, 1691/2, dated February 12.
2. *The Gentleman's Journal* for April, 1692, dated April 12; Luttrell, II, 413.
3. On April 16 Luttrell (II, 422) records that it "has been acted with applause."

Cleomenes achieved a success which justified Dryden's opinion that it "*was capable of moving Compassion on the Stage.*"

Mountfort again spoke the prologue, which contained an appeal to the women in the audience. Here they are entreated either to discard the Foplings who are fond of farce or to teach them how manly passions ought to move. The latter task, however, appears hopeless:

> *You can make Fools of Wits, we find each Hour,*
> *But to make Wits of Fools, is past your Power.*

Although "the fair" could not perform that miracle, they were ready to give the play a kind reception, for which the author acknowledged that he was particularly grateful.

Dryden also praised the actors for the justice which they did him in the performance of their parts. And well he might, for *Cleomenes* was presented with the complete strength of the tragedians of the company. Mrs. Betterton appeared as Cratesiclea, the true Spartan mother of the hero, and Mrs. Bracegirdle played his second wife Cleora. Young Michael Lee was his fifteen-year-old son Cleonidas. Alexander essayed the youthful and easily flattered king of Egypt, Ptolemy, and Sandford acted Sosibius, the crafty minister of state. Pantheus, the true friend who falls upon his sword after Cleomenes' death, was taken by Kynaston.

But the most important rôles were in the hands of the triad. Betterton, of course, played the name character — the unfortunate Spartan ruler who, after being defeated in battle, takes refuge in Egypt, and arouses the love of the king's mistress, Cassandra. Because of his indifference she becomes angry and has him thrown into prison to starve.

After repeated and vain efforts on her part to persuade
him to accept her and after the deaths of his wife, mother,
and son, he and his friend Cleanthes agree to kill each
other, and they die in each other's arms. The acting of
Mrs. Barry as the thwarted Cassandra called forth the
greatest enthusiasm of the author, who was ready to say
"*what the Town has generally granted, That Mrs.* Barry,
always Excellent, has, in this Tragedy, *excell'd Herself, and
gain'd a Reputation beyond any Woman whom* [*he had*]
ever seen on the Theatre." To Mountfort was assigned the
noble-minded Egyptian Cleanthes, the captain of the
guard, who is disgusted with his country because it is
swayed by such an effeminate tyrant as Ptolemy. In
order to save Cleomenes he lets him think he is false, but
later persuades him of his loyalty by bringing him food
in prison and giving him the contents of a vial which
prevent him from fainting. After the two men are unable
either to arouse the slothful Egyptians or to meet their
deaths during the uprising, they are ready to accept their
fate at each other's hands.

Possibly because of the success of *Cleomenes* the company was willing to act another tragedy before the summer. During the week of June 6, they again gave a play
with its scene laid in the ancient world, *Regulus* by John
Crowne.[1] Described as a "Tragedy . . . intermixed with
a vein of Comedy," it did not have the good fortune of its
predecessor, for, as Gildon says, it "met with no very good
Success."[2]

Betterton was once more the hero whose name gave the

1. *The Gentleman's Journal* for June, 1692, dated June 17, says *Regulus* "was
acted the last week."
2. P. 30.

title to the tragedy. Again he depicted nobility of character as the Roman consul who, after being taken prisoner by the Carthaginians, is allowed to go on an embassy to his camp, where he urges his countrymen to continue fighting. Then, despite the pleadings to remain behind, he returns to the city of the enemy and to certain death. Mrs. Barry played Fulvia, the lover of Regulus, a part which called for what she had presented many times in tragedies with Betterton — vain pleadings, fears, and madness.

In the secondary plot Mountfort had a rôle which enabled him to hold the center of the stage as often as Betterton and Mrs. Barry. He delineated the young and ambitious Asdrubal who wishes to overthrow the commonwealth of Carthage and make himself king, apparently only because he has tried all pleasures except reigning. For a time it seems likely that he may be successful in his attempt, but he is finally exposed and placed under arrest. It is pleasant to think that in the last part which he was to act in a new play Mountfort had scenes with Leigh and Underhill, with whom he had formerly appeared in many a rollicking comedy. These two actors and Doggett, who now was ready to assume characters that twelve months before would have been taken by Nokes, portrayed the three conspirators against the government of Carthage who were willing to further the ambitions of Asdrubal, provided of course that they receive ample rewards, and who are hanged after they have been repudiated by the conscienceless young Carthaginian. Leigh was cast for the rich senator Gisgon who prides himself on being a man of quality and boasts that he has never done good to one of the vulgar in his life. Underhill represented the priest with "a rubrick Nose, and a canonical belly," Hiarbas; and Doggett, who had clearly established himself in public esteem by his excellent acting of comic bits in plays by D'Urfey, had the rôle of the treacherous citizen Batto, who flatters all sides for profits and is not only willing to sell arms to the Romans, but is also anticipating the disposal of corn at a higher price to his starving countrymen, should the siege of the city continue.

As an offset to these parts of traitors taken by the comedians, the other actors who usually met the demands of the tragic repertoire acted characters more apt to win the sympathies of the audience. Kynaston again played the father as the pro-consul Metellus, who begs his daughter Fulvia not to plead with her lover to remain. Sandford, whom the patrons of the theatre were accustomed to find exulting in villainies, appeared as Hamilcar, the prince of the Carthaginian senate, who opposes the ambitions of Asdrubal and acts as hostage for Regulus when the Roman goes on his errand. Williams was the lover of Hamilcar's daughter, the Spartan Xantippus, who for a time leads the Carthaginian army, but who, when Regulus is tortured unto death, goes over to the enemy.

XV

In addition to the many new parts he created during the last four years of his life, Mountfort also at this time played rôles which had formerly been acted by other persons. Cibber was especially enthusiastic about his performance of Sparkish in *The Country Wife*. The deluded fop, who through refusing to appear jealous loses his love Alithea, offered much to the actor who could play "the brisk, vain, rude, and lively Coxcomb, the false, flashy Pretender to

Wit, and the Dupe of his own Sufficiency." In this rôle Mountfort followed Jo Haynes, but about who in the United Company of 1690 succeeded Hart, Mohun, Mrs. Boutell, and Mrs. Knepp as Horner, Pinchwife, Margery, and Lady Fidget, the records are unfortunately silent.

It is a far cry from Sparkish to Macduff, but Mountfort excelled in both parts. The Restoration Macduff in D'Avenant's perversion occupies the stage more often than his Elizabethan prototype, and shares with his wife several scenes not found in the original. With her he listens to songs by the witches and to prophecies concerning their future; and by her, in a passage written in heroic couplets, he is warned against ambition. What Cibber was to remember of Mountfort's Macduff fifty years later was not the reading of these interpolated lines, but the happy skill and grace displayed in "two Scenes, the one of Terror, in the second Act, and the other of Compassion, in the fourth," [1] both of which belong largely to Shakespeare's text. When Mountfort played Macduff, Macbeth and Lady Macbeth were acted by the Bettertons, who had held these rôles since the opening of the theatres after the Restoration.

It is possible also that sometime between 1689 and 1691 Mountfort appeared in a revival of that delightful comedy of unknown authorship, *The Merry Devil of Edmonton*. Unfortunately we have not the authority of Cibber, Downes, or a printed cast in a contemporary quarto to assist us here. The suggestion that there was such a performance was made by Collier, who found a cast with the names of actors belonging to the United Company written opposite the parts "on the back of a copy of the edition of

1. II, 228–229.

1655, in the Garrick Collection, in a hand no doubt of the time when it was again brought upon the stage." [1] There is no knowing whether these notations represent the actual casting for an actual performance or whether a frequenter of the playhouse, after reading the comedy, amused himself for an idle hour by assigning the various parts to the actors who appeared best fitted for them. Mountfort's name is opposite the character of Raymond Mounchensey. With Mountfort as the lover, Mrs. Bracegirdle seems an almost inevitable choice as Millicent, with whom he elopes. Sandford is down for the father, Sir Arthur Clare, and Kynaston for the merry devil Fabel. But what makes one inclined to question the authority of this cast is the fact that to Betterton is given the comparatively unimportant rôle of Sir Ralph Jerningham. In no other play of this time of which we have authentic information does he act a part of such comparative insignificance.

The statement that Mountfort played Castalio in *The Orphan* [2] is also not based on absolutely conclusive evidence. Cibber and Downes again make no mention of the fact. The authority for the attribution is probably a sentence in the *Dramatic Miscellanies* of Thomas Davies, a work published nearly one hundred years after the actor's death:

Cibber has told us, that the Castalio of Betterton was superior to all the performances he had ever seen of the character; though he confessed, at the same time, that he was not so eminent in representing lovers, from person and elocution, as parts which required less softness. Mountfort, a younger man, who

1. *A Select Collection of Old English Plays originally published by Robert Dodsley* (ed. W. C. Hazlitt, London, 1875), X, 204.
2. Genest, II, 35, lists Castalio among Mountfort's parts.

succeeded him, being endowed by nature with a handsome person, a most melodious voice, and pleasing address, was, at least to the female part of the audience, which I think best qualified to distinguish, rather nearer to the idea of an accomplished and successful lover.[1]

These words are obviously suggested by Cibber's accounts of the two actors with the added implication that Mountfort succeeded Betterton in the rôle. If Mountfort did for a time appear as Castalio, his Monimia was of course Mrs. Barry, for whom Otway had drawn the character. One wonders whether he played with her on February 9, 1692,[2] when the tragedy was given before the queen and the maids of honor, and also whether he was Castalio at the performance when Cibber acted the Chaplain so well that Cardell Goodman clapped him on the shoulder the next day and said, "*If he does not make a good Actor, I'll be d——'d.*"[3] We have no definite evidence, however, that Mountfort appeared on these occasions, and it may well be that Betterton did not relinquish the part of the distressed lover to the younger man.

There is not much more to be said of the last months of Mountfort's life. We have one brief glimpse: on September 26, "after a long contention between M![r] Betterton

1. Thomas Davies, *Dramatic Miscellanies* (London, 1784), III, 206. Davies bases his statement on these remarks of Cibber: "*Betterton* had a Voice of that kind which gave more Spirit to Terror than to the softer Passions; of more Strength than Melody. The Rage and Jealousy of *Othello* became him better than the Sighs and Tenderness of *Castalio*: For though in *Castalio* he only excell'd others, in *Othello* he excell'd himself" (I, 116); "Of Person he [i.e. Mountfort] was tall, well made, fair, and of an agreeable Aspect: His Voice clear, full, and melodious: In Tragedy he was the most affecting Lover within my Memory" (I, 127).

2. L.C. 5/151, p. 369 (Nicoll, p. 314).

3. *Apology*, I, 183.

Mr Mountfort Mr Leigh & others ye Priviledges of ye shar-
ing Actors were setled to all their contents & satisfacōns
And entered into y̆ Day Booke as may there appear." [1]
But the Day Book has not yet come to light, and so the
details of the transaction are for the present lost.

About six weeks after these privileges were settled, the
company acted their first new play of the season of 1692–
1693. Again a tragedy but based upon English rather than
classical history, it was from the pen of the surgeon John
Bancroft, whose *Edward III* had two years before been a
present to Mountfort. By November 21 *Henry II, King
of England; With the Death of Rosamond* had been "acted
several times with applause." [2] The rôles of the royal lover
and the fair Rosamond were taken by Betterton and Mrs.
Bracegirdle, the jealous Queen Eleanor by Mrs. Barry.
Sandford had a long part as the villainous Abbot who is
ever on the alert to thwart the King. Leigh and Doggett,
as the pander Sir Thomas Vaughan and the priest Ber-
trard, again played semi-comic characters, who in the last
act were required to meet their deaths. The only other
rôle of importance, the courtier Verulam, was given to
Kynaston.

Betterton's playing King Henry probably explains the
absence of Mountfort from the cast; but when the tragedy
came off the press in the latter part of the month of its first
performance, it, like *Edward III*, was published anony-
mously and was preceded by a dedication written by the

1. L.C. 7/3.
2. *The Gentleman's Journal* for October, 1692, which was advertised in *The
London Gazette* of November 21–24. Its second performance took place on November 9. See W. J. Lawrence, *The Elizabethan Playhouse and Other Studies*, 2d
series (Stratford upon Avon, 1913), p. 240. It was seen by the queen and maids
of honor on November 14.

actor. In the epistle addressed to "the Truly Worthy Sir *THOMAS COOKE* Kt. *Alderman, and Sheriff of the Most Famous City of* LONDON" and signed "*Your Most Obedient Servant,* WILL. MOUNTFORT," the player, although a stranger to the knight, praises his generosity in giving fire and food to the poor during the hard frost, and in helping the distressed Irish Protestants.[1] One would like to know whether Sir Thomas was pleased with this recognition of his charity and whether he responded with a present to the dedicator. The response in this instance would have had to be prompt if the actor was to enjoy any benefit from it, for in less than two weeks after the printed play was advertised in *The London Gazette*[2] Mountfort was dead.

1. Early in October, 1690, Luttrell mentions that Cook "has lately given 500 *l.* to help carry over the Irish protestants into Ireland, who had not wherewith to goe over." On February 13, 1692, he records that Cook was chosen alderman of London "in room of Sir John Lawrence, deceased." On June 24 he and Sir Thomas Lane were unanimously chosen sheriffs of London; and on September 28 they entered on their offices (II, 112, 357, 493, 578).

2. No. 2822 (November 24–28, 1692).

PART II

DEATH

PART II

Death

I

AMONG the frequenters of the playhouse during the latter part of 1692 was Charles, fourth Lord Mohun of Okehampton,[1] then aged fifteen, who was later to win notoriety as a duelist and to furnish Thackeray with a villain for *Henry Esmond*. He was often in the company of Captain Richard Hill,[2] at least five years his senior, the son of a former dean of Kilkenny. After four years' service in the regiments of Adam Loftus, Viscount Lisburne, and Colonel Thomas Erle in the Irish war and the campaigns in Flanders, Hill had come to London. But now Venus had usurped the place of Mars, and he hoped in vain to be received as lover by

1. The story of the death of Mountfort has been told many times, most recently by Robert S. Forsythe in *A Noble Rake: The Life of Charles, Fourth Lord Mohun* (Cambridge, Massachusetts, 1928). In his fully documented second chapter Mr. Forsythe has indicated the shortcomings of many of the earlier accounts, which incorrectly assume that Mohun was the murderer of the actor. An accurate narrative of the circumstances surrounding Mountfort's death is also found in Dutton Cook, *Hours with the Players* (London, 1881), I, 1–37. Cook and Forsythe have used as the basis of their accounts the report of the trial of Mohun published by command of the House of Peers in 1693. In my retelling of the events of December 9, 1692, and of the happenings of the preceding week, I have drawn heavily from the same source of information. I have also made use of a manuscript hitherto neglected by writers on the subject. The material in MS. Egerton 2623, fols. 46–49, which is described in Appendix C, does not contradict the facts appearing in the published report of the trial; it simply adds details which assist in giving vividness to the story.

2. See Appendix D.

Mrs. Bracegirdle. Since his ardor was unable to win the actress, he concluded that Mountfort, whom he undoubtedly had seen appear with her more than once upon the stage, was in some manner responsible for her coldness.

On Friday, December 2, Mohun attended a performance of *The Rival Queens* with a Mr. Brereton. At supper afterwards he praised the play and commended particularly Mountfort's Alexander. Brereton thought that Mountfort had never acted so well in his life as on this occasion; he felt, however, that the actor was at his best in comedy and would never make so good a tragedian as Betterton or some others. Mohun then expressed a desire to drink a bottle of wine with him, for Mountfort had treated him civilly when several other players had been rude, "more than their Business did require of them." Brereton, who had been in the actor's company once, was not enthusiastic and replied to the young lord, "I do not think him worth you[r] Acquaintance, but you may do what you will." On the following Tuesday, Mohun went to Brereton's lodgings and told how the night before Mountfort had again treated him better at the playhouse than the other actors, and he repeated his desire of drinking a bottle of wine with him. He also declared: "I am going about some Business to *Kensington*, but within a day or two you shall certainly hear of me, and we will fix a time for it, and if I do not like his Company, I will never trouble you nor my self more with it."

Although these sentiments concerning the actor which Brereton attributed to Mohun at the trial were friendly, what was said by Hill to various members of the company during the week following December 2 was far from amicable. On one occasion when Hill and George Powell were together, the conversation turned on Mrs. Bracegirdle, and her health was drunk. Then the captain, after declaring that Mountfort was the only bar between him and the actress, said he was determined to be revenged. A few days later, Powell was supping with Mohun, Hill, and Colonel Tredenham,[1] and the name of Mrs. Bracegirdle was again mentioned. Hill whispered to Powell, "I am resolved to have the Blood of *Mountfort*." Powell replied that he did not think it right to speak that way behind a gentleman's back to one who was his friend, and, furthermore, that he would acquaint Mountfort with what had been said. He had no doubt that Mountfort would give satisfaction for any injury done Hill. Another time, the actor John Hodgson[2] supped at the Rose Tavern in Covent Garden with the two friends. The talk soon arrived at the inevitable subject; and Hill averred that he did not doubt he would be successful in his love for Mrs. Bracegirdle, were it not for Mountfort, whom "I design to be the Death of." When Powell and Hodgson were later to be summoned as witnesses at the trial of Mohun, they could not recall whether his lordship made any reply or took any notice of Hill's threat.

Not all the captain's confidants were among the male members of the company. More than once he had talked with Mrs. Knight concerning his love. About four days before the fatal encounter, Hill told her that he was satisfied Mrs. Bracegirdle hated him. Mrs. Knight replied that

1. Possibly Sir Joseph Tredenham, who on April 30, 1686, and again on December 26, 1690, had been commissioned captain and keeper of St. Mawes Castle, Cornwall (Dalton, *English Army Lists*, II, 72, III, 162).
2. His name is spelled "Hudson" in the published *Tryal*; in casts in contemporary quartos it appears as "Hudson," "Hodson," "Hodgsdon," and "Hodgson," the latter most frequently.

she did not believe she hated anybody or loved anybody. To this remark Hill answered that she did love somebody, but he had thought of a way to be even with that person. On Wednesday, the seventh, he again went to the play-house and once more met Mrs. Knight as she was coming out of the dressing-room. He begged her to deliver a letter to Mrs. Bracegirdle, but she refused on the ground that Mrs. Bracegirdle, because she hated Hill, would not love anybody who spoke for him, and Mrs. Knight had no desire to create enemies for herself in the house, since she had some already. Hill demanded, "What Enemies, *Mountfort* do you mean?" and then after an oath, he concluded, "I shall find a way with him speedily."

On the very day that Hill had tried to persuade Mrs. Knight to play the messenger, Mohun fought a duel with Lord Kennedy, in which each of the opponents was reported wounded. The fact that the two had challenged each other as the result of a drunken quarrel a week or so before had reached the ears of King William, who confined them to their lodgings. An attempt was then made by Daniel Finch, Earl of Nottingham, to patch up the disagreement, but it proved fruitless, and so they met.[1] Possibly the contemplated duel was the "Business" at Kensington, to which Mohun had referred in his conversation with Brereton. Mohun's wound could not have been serious, for he was ready on Friday to aid Hill in his adventure. The nights of Wednesday and Thursday, it appears, were spent by his lordship at his friend's lodgings in Buckingham Court.

1. Luttrell, II, 628–629, 631, 636; *Correspondence of the Family of Hatton*, ed. Edward M. Thompson (Camden Society), II, 187.

II

Friday, December 9, was the day selected for the abduction of Mrs. Bracegirdle, and so in the morning Hill began to make his preparations. He requested his landlady, Mrs. Ann Rudd, to lend him a suit of night linen and a gown. At first unwilling, she finally agreed to provide him with the linen only. The two friends drove to the stables of William Dixon, who for thirty shillings was to furnish the necessary conveyance. A pair of horses and coach were to be at the playhouse and to be driven from there to the Strand and then to the "pound's end." Here four other horses were to be in readiness to draw the coach to its destination at Totteridge. The men also visited the theatre. After the rehearsal, Mrs. Bracegirdle noticed that Hill was watching her, and so she hid until she was found by Mohun. She managed, however, to make her escape; and for nearly an hour afterwards Hill kept guard at one door and Mohun at another.

They dined with Mrs. Elizabeth Sandys, a person apparently of dubious reputation, at the Three Tuns in Chandos Street.[1] She was unable to enlighten Mohun about how intimate Mountfort had been with Mrs. Bracegirdle. In the course of the conversation, Mohun remarked that this design would cost Hill fifty guineas. The belligerent captain then threatened to stab "the Villain" if he should offer any resistance, and his lordship said he would stand by his friend. At this time Hill desired an acquaintance to borrow a case of pistols for him from Captain Leister; he did not care to ask for them himself, feeling

1. "Shandois-street" in the *Tryal*.

certain that they would not be lent if the owner knew to what use they were to be put. Before the friends parted, Mohun declared, upon his word and honor, that he would be at the playhouse by six. In the afternoon, Hill again went to his lodgings, took the linen and a night-gown, and asked Mrs. Rudd to lend him a pair of pistols, but she had none.

At the appointed hour, the two were at the theatre. They went into the scene-room, where Hodgson saw them exchanging their coats, probably for the purpose of confusing any persons who might be witnesses of the abduction. John Rogers asked them, when they came out of the pit upon the stage, for the overplus of money that was due. One of them insolently refused to pay it and threatened to do violence to any of the masters of the house whom Rogers might summon. Not finding Mrs. Bracegirdle, they left the building.

According to the plan, Dixon was ready with his coach and pair near the Horseshoe Tavern in Drury Lane. After a time he drove Mohun and Hill to Norfolk Street. Here they left the conveyance and went to the White Horse Tavern and probably also to the actress's lodgings on Howard Street, where they learned that she was at Mr. Gawen Page's house on Princes Street for supper. The coachman overheard Hill say, "We are Betrayed. Damme, my Lord, let us go and Thresh him." They were then driven back to Drury Lane where the coach took its stand near Lord Craven's residence. The two friends proceeded to the Horseshoe Tavern, where, so Hill's footboy Thomas Lake (or Leake) was later to testify, they were joined by Mrs. Bracegirdle's brother Hamlet, who drank with them and agreed to inform them when the actress left Mr. Page's house and which way she was to go home.

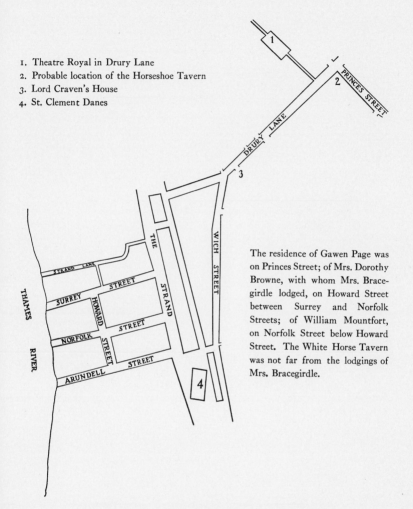

1. Theatre Royal in Drury Lane
2. Probable location of the Horseshoe Tavern
3. Lord Craven's House
4. St. Clement Danes

The residence of Gawen Page was on Princes Street; of Mrs. Dorothy Browne, with whom Mrs. Bracegirdle lodged, on Howard Street between Surrey and Norfolk Streets; of William Mountfort, on Norfolk Street below Howard Street. The White Horse Tavern was not far from the lodgings of Mrs. Bracegirdle.

THE SCENE OF THE EVENTS OF DECEMBER 9, 1692

About ten o'clock, Mrs. Bracegirdle, her mother and brother, accompanied by Mr. Page, proceeded down Princes Street and turned into Drury Lane on the half-mile walk to the lodgings of the Bracegirdles at Mrs. Dorothy Browne's on Howard Street. As they approached Lord Craven's door, two soldiers, who had been previously instructed by the captain, stepped forward, parted the actress from Page, and attempted to thrust her into the coach. Four or five others came up, and in the ensuing tussle nearly knocked the mother down; but Mrs. Martha Bracegirdle quickly recovered her footing and clung to her daughter so that they were unable to accomplish their design. In the meantime, Hill had drawn his sword and, crying, "You Villain, Stand," had attacked Page. One of the strokes was aimed at his opponent's head, but it was warded off. By his skill at receiving blows upon his cane, Page escaped unharmed. Because of the noise caused by the crying out of the actress and the shouts for assistance by Page, a crowd gathered, and the abductors soon realized that their plans were thwarted.

Hill then took by the hand Mrs. Bracegirdle, who was apparently about to faint, and said he would escort her home. With him on one side and her mother on the other, they walked down Drury Lane. Mohun, who during the scuffle had remained seated in the coach, — possibly he had not thoroughly recovered from the wound of two days before, — now came out and followed. The soldiers did the same, but they were soon dismissed by the captain, who, since his scabbard had been lost in the mêlée, carried his drawn sword and threatened to be revenged.

In a few minutes they had crossed the Strand and were at Mrs. Browne's door in Howard Street. As they were entering the house, Hill pulled Page by the sleeve and asked to speak with him. Page replied that tomorrow would serve. Hill then answered, "Well, *To Morrow then; but, God Damn me, you will not go out to Night.*"

After the elder Mrs. Bracegirdle had removed her hood and scarf, she returned to the door and asked the men their business. The conversation which followed was overheard by the servant at a neighboring house, Ann Knevitt, who reported at the trial that they replied that they wished to beg her daughter's pardon for what they had done. The mother then began to abuse them and said she believed that they had come to rob her daughter. The response was that they were there upon a very honorable design. She countered this answer with a statement that they should have come honorably at a seasonable time. One of them asserted that it was not an unseasonable time, for she herself was out of doors then. Finally, after much wrangling, she went inside the house.

When the actress entered the room crying, Mrs. Browne inquired what was the matter. Upon learning the cause, she also went to the door, and, seeing the two men walking up and down before the house, she asked if they were the persons who had used Mrs. Bracegirdle in this manner. Mohun replied that he had protected her: "*if it had not been for me, the Rabble would have torn her a pieces; for if we had had a mind to carry her away, we had six or seven Pistols Charged in the Coach, and could easily have suppressed the Tumult.*" His design, he continued, had been only to serve his friend, who had intended to take Mrs. Bracegirdle out of town, keep her for a week, and see if he could persuade her to marry him. Hill's words were more threatening: "*I shall light on this* Mountfort." Mrs. Browne asked what hurt Mountfort had done him, and he replied, "*I have been Abused, and I will be Revenged.*" Shortly afterwards, she went to the home of the actor, which was around the corner on Norfolk Street, and told his wife what had been said.

After Mrs. Martha Bracegirdle had finished her conversation with the men, she entered the parlor and informed her daughter that the two were still at the door and that Hill desired permission to beg her pardon. The loquacious maid, Elizabeth Walker, was ready with the suggestion that if her mistress gave her leave she would go outside and demand the captain's sword. Then he might come in and beg her pardon — an act which would prevent a great deal of danger. But Mrs. Martha called her a prating slut for her pains, and Mrs. Anne said that if he begged her pardon upon his knees, she would neither forgive him nor see him again.

The younger woman then sent her brother and the maid to Mountfort's house to see whether the actor was in safety. When word was brought that he was not there, Mrs. Bracegirdle ordered the maid to return and to urge Mrs. Mountfort to warn her husband not to come home without a good guard because Mohun and Hill were walking about the street. Mrs. Mountfort's maid, accompanied by Elizabeth Walker, straightway visited several taverns looking for the actor, but their search proved fruitless. In the meantime, the anxious group around Mrs. Bracegirdle was augmented by Mrs. Page, who, upon learning of her husband's encounter with the would-be abductors, had hurried to Mrs. Browne's.

While the search for Mountfort was in progress, Mohun and Hill continued to walk back and forth on Howard

Street. Richard Row (or Rose),[1] who lived in the adjoining Surrey Street, heard the noise and went outdoors to ascertain what was the matter. He was later to testify that he saw two gentlemen and two boys and that one of the latter held one of the gentlemen by the arm and said, "*Pray my Lord, Good my Lord, don't do it, alter your Resolution.*" To these words came the reply that they would be revenged that night or to-morrow. At the trial of Mohun no corroborative evidence was brought forth, and Thomas Lake, Hill's boy, who was not under oath, denied that he either said or heard these words.[2]

Hill was persistent in wishing the actress to come but to the hatch that he might see her and beg her pardon. If she did not give him this opportunity, he said, they would walk there all night. Because it was becoming very cold, one of the friends called to the boy to bring him his cloak, but he decided not to wear it since his companion was not similarly provided. After a time, the drawer from the Horseshoe Tavern supplied them with a bottle of canary.[3] This they drank in the street and pledged the health of the actress. They were heard to ask a gentleman whether he would join them in a glass of wine; and they also considered walking in front of Mrs. Barry's window.

After the two had sauntered back and forth for nearly

1. "Row" in the published *Tryal*; "Rose" in journal of the House of Lords.

2. Elizabeth Walker, who was not under oath, said at the trial that there was a discourse in the street "that Captain *Hill* had made a Vow that he would kill himself that Night, and that my Lord *Mohun*, having a Respect for him, watched to prevent him from doing himself a Mischief."

3. Thomas Leak (*sic*) in information taken upon oath on December 10 deposed: "My L[d] and y[e] Cap[tn] Stayd in the Street there about an hour and halfe., And Sent this Inform[t] to the white Horse Taverne where they had been before., They went [sent?] to y[e] Horse Shoe Taverne for a Bottle of Canary and the Drawer brought it, and My L[d] and y[e] Cap[tn] Dranck of it in the Street."

an hour and a half, it chanced that the constable John
Davenport, as he was making his rounds along the Strand,
had divided the watch of eight or ten men into two groups,
one to proceed down Strand Lane under his leadership and
the other to accompany his beadle, William Merry, along
Surrey Street. As Merry turned into Howard Street, Hill
and Mohun approached him on the paved stones with
their swords drawn. The challenge was given, "Who
comes there?" And Mohun replied, "A Friend." The
beadle then ordered them to return their swords and to
stand off. Mohun, declaring he was a peer of the land,
offered his weapon, but Merry did not take it. Instead, he
said, "God Bless your Honor my Lord, *I* know not what
you are, but *I* hope you are doing no harm."

Thomas Fennel, one of Merry's group, seeing that there
might be trouble, at once summoned the constable, who
soon appeared with the other watchmen. Mrs. Browne
then stepped outside her house and called to the new-
comers to secure the men. Mohun offered his sword very
civilly to the constable — so Davenport testified — and
said that he was a peer of the realm. Mrs. Bracegirdle, who
was listening at the door to what was going on, was, however, to recall at the trial that Mohun added, "Touch me
if you dare." [1] Hill explained that he was carrying his
sword because he had lost his scabbard in Drury Lane.
James Bassit, another of the watchmen, remembered that
when the two men were asked what they were doing there,
they replied that they were drinking a bottle of wine and

1. Mrs. Browne testified also to this effect on December 10: "this Inform.^t
call'd the Watch to Secure them and the Watch Endeavouring to Seize them the
S.^d Lord Mohun Said he was a Peer of the Realm and let ye watch touch Him if
they Durst." At the trial she did not mention Mohun's threat.

that Hill added, "You may knock me down if you please."
To this invitation Bassit responded, "Nay, we never use to
knock any Gentlemen down, unless there be occasion."

The constable and the beadle questioned the people
standing in the street and were told that one of the men
had a sweetheart there and that he wanted to speak to her.
Learning that the two had been at the White Horse Tavern
earlier in the evening, the watch went at once to that place
to find out more concerning the matter. There they received the information that the men had been drinking.

III

Apparently not long after the watch had left for the
White Horse Tavern, Sir John Shorter was walking down
Norfolk Street to his house. It was probably as he passed
Howard Street that Mohun stepped up, mistook him for
the actor, and embraced him, saying, "Dear Mountfort!"
But the error was at once discovered, and Shorter went on
to his destination.[1] A few minutes afterwards, Mountfort
appeared from the same direction. Instead of passing the
corner of the cross street and continuing the short distance

1. The anecdote, which is quoted in *Notes and Queries*, 1st series, II, 516,
appears in *Walpoliana*, 2d ed., II, 96: "Mr. Shorter, my mother's father, was
walking down Norfolk-street in the Strand, to his house there, just before poor
Mountfort the player was killed in that street, by assassins hired by Lord
Mohun. This nobleman, lying in wait for his prey, came up and embraced Mr.
Shorter by mistake, saying, "Dear Mountfort!" It was fortunate that he was
instantly undeceived, for Mr. Shorter had hardly reached his house before the
murder took place."

Forsythe, p. 29, calls attention to certain errors of fact which do not add to
the credibility of the anecdote: that Mountfort was attacked in Howard Street,
not Norfolk Street, and that he was not assailed by assassins hired by Mohun.
One may accept as errors what was stated to have taken place after the meeting
and still believe that Shorter reported correctly what happened as he passed the
corner of Howard and Norfolk Streets.

to his own door, he turned into Howard Street. Mrs. Browne recognized him at once and hurried to meet him. She took him by the hand and told him she would speak with him, but the actor ignored her entreaties and pressed on to where the two friends were standing. John [or Edward] Warington,[1] an observer of what was taking place, said that Mountfort was carrying his sword in the scabbard;[2] upon questioning by Mohun at the trial, Mrs. Browne believed the sword was by his side.

Mohun embraced Mountfort, and the two addressed each other in terms of respect. When Mohun made reference to the thwarted abduction and asked if he had been sent for, Mountfort disclaimed any knowledge of the business, saying that he had come there by chance. He would know if his wife had disobliged his lordship. If so, she should ask his pardon; but Mrs. Bracegirdle was no concern of his. Mrs. Brewer, who was watching the proceedings from Mrs. Browne's door, was to testify that Hill attempted to draw Mohun away, saying, *"Pray my Lord, hold your Tongue, this is not a convenient time to discourse this Business."* Mountfort made a remark reported variously by witnesses from the comparatively mild, "I hope your Lordship will not vindicate Mr. *Hill* in any such Action as this" to the more severe statement that "it was a Dishonour to him to keep Company with Captain *Hill*."

What occurred next happened in a shorter time than it

1. "Edward" in the published *Tryal*; "John" in the journal of the House of Lords and the manuscript depositions.

2. Warington, who was not under oath at the trial, made this statement "to the best of [his] Knowledge." On December 10, however, he made no statement concerning Mountfort's having his sword in his hand. Lake, on December 10, deposed upon oath that Mountfort had "his Sword Ouer his Arm," and at the trial he alleged that Mountfort "carried his Sword in his Hand."

takes to relate. Again the eye-witnesses — Mrs. Browne, her neighbor Mrs. Brewer, the captain's footboy Lake, and the maids, Elizabeth Walker and Ann Jones — are not in perfect agreement. Two of them were to testify that Hill struck Mountfort a box on the ear, at which the actor demanded, "*Damme, what's that for?*" Lake, whose occupation would probably not have made him entirely unprejudiced, related that Hill came up, after Mountfort had spoken of him to Mohun, and uttered words which seem unusually calm, "*if you have any thing to say to me, I can Vindicate my self, and pray now Draw.*"

Mrs. Brewer said that Hill made a pass at the actor, who did not have his sword drawn. Mrs. Browne recalled that Mountfort drew his sword, but she could not tell whether he did so before or after he received his wound. It was also reported that the men made two or three passes at each other in the middle of the street. In the course of the fighting, Mountfort's sword was broken and the actor exclaimed, after Hill's weapon had pierced his body, "I am a dead Man." All this time Mohun stood on the paved stones near the house, made no effort to interfere, and said, as Lake was to swear before the coroner, that he would stand by his friend.

Warington, when he saw that there was likely to be shedding of blood, went inside his dwelling to get a paring-shovel with which to part the men. Ann Knevitt, who was warming a bed in an upstairs room at Mrs. Brewer's, hearing the noise in the street below, looked out and became so frightened at seeing the sword in Mountfort's body that she nearly fell from the window. One of the persons in the street, when he heard why she was so terrified, shouted: "Will you break your Neck for that Reason? It may be it is one of the Watchmen." Hill drew his sword from the body of his opponent and ran as fast as he could up Surrey Street, and Mountfort moved as well as he was able towards his home.

As soon as the blow was struck, Mrs. Brewer had called "*Murder.*" The shouts were heard by Mrs. Page, who a short time before had gone to the house of the Mountforts in order again to urge Mrs. Mountfort to send a warning to her husband. She opened the door and was confronted by the bleeding actor. He came in, fell with his arms about her neck to steady himself, and said that Hill had murdered him.

In the meantime, Elizabeth Walker picked up the actor's sword, noticed that a good-sized piece of it was broken off, and handed it to some people who were standing near Mrs. Browne's door. Mohun wished her to bear witness that he had no hand in Mountfort's death. She replied, "No, my Lord, I think you have not." By the time that Warington returned to the street with the shovel, both the fighters had disappeared. When he asked which way they had gone, Mohun turned about and for a moment Warington was afraid. He heard his lordship declare, "Here am I. I did not offer to oppose or draw my Sword, you all know it."

Now Mrs. Page, who had helped Mountfort to his parlor door where he fell down, came into the street crying, "Murder." Mohun walked towards her and wished her to take notice that he was guiltless for his sword was not drawn. But she let him know that a short time before (that is, when she went to warn Mrs. Mountfort) she had seen him in "Mr. *Hill*'s Company with his naked Sword."

The watch then arrived. Their investigations at the White Horse Tavern concerning the persons who had made the disturbance in the street had been interrupted by the shouts of "Murder." Mrs. Page bade the constable Davenport, who reached Howard Street before his less nimble-footed comrade Merry, to secure Mohun. Upon surrendering his sword, his lordship begged to be used like a gentleman. As Bassit, one of the watchmen, took him by the sleeve, he "shook and quak'd and trembled."

By the time he had arrived at the Round House, where he passed the night, he had regained his composure. He, who during the fighting had declared that he would stand by his friend, now asked if Hill was taken. Davenport replied in the negative and added, "This is a bad misfortune you are happen'd into." Mohun answered: "*God Damme, I am glad he is not Taken, but I am sorry he has no more Mony about him; I wish he had some of mine; and, I do not care a Farthing if I am Hang'd for him.*" He informed them that he and Hill had changed their coats several times that day, and also told them where his friend's lodgings were.

Davenport and the watch then proceeded to the captain's quarters in Buckingham Court. As they were conducting their search, the footboy Lake, who had followed his master in fleeing from Howard Street but who had lost him in the neighborhood of Covent Garden, returned to their rooms and was arrested. Gunpowder and ball were found upon him.

To return to the victim of Hill's anger. When Gawen Page heard the cry of "Murder," he left Mrs. Browne's house and went out on the street where he saw Mohun surrender himself to the constable. Then he hurried to Mountfort's home and found the actor lying in his blood upon the parlor floor. The wounded man, who recognized his visitor, begged to be lifted up, and, to Page's question whether he had had time to defend himself, he replied that he had been barbarously run through before he could draw his sword.

The surgeon, John Bancroft, in whose plays *Edward III* and *Henry II* Mountfort had been interested, was immediately summoned to Norfolk Street; and after an examination revealed a wound on the right side one inch broad and twenty inches deep, he informed the actor of his hopeless condition.[1] The fellow-player, George Powell, who was on hand while Mountfort was still lying on the parlor floor, remained with the dying man all night after he had been put to bed. Powell, like Page, inquired how he had been wounded and was told that Mountfort did not draw his sword until after he had received his wound and that Hill had run him through while Mohun was talking to him.

Bancroft attended his patient until four o'clock; when he returned at eight, he found in attendance Mr. Hobbs,[2] who corroborated his opinion concerning the actor. Before he departed near ten to appear before the justices at Hicks Hall, he said to the man whose pulse was "Intermitting and Languid" and who was "in a cold faint and clammy Sweat and alsoe convulsive": "*I* suppose where *I* am going, *I* shall be asked some Questions about what you may have

1. On December 10 Bancroft testified that Mountfort was "very Desperately wounded on ye right Side of his Belly near the Short ribbe"; at the trial he said that he found Mountfort "very desperately Wounded; it went in and out by his Back-bone, behind his left Side." In the indictment of Mohun, the wound is said to have been "*of the breadth of one Inch, and of the depth of twenty Inches*" on the "*Right side of the Body . . . near the . . . Right Pap.*"

2. Congreve, in a letter to Tonson, dated August 20 [1695], writes, "I am very glad that you have had so much satisfaction in the country & that Dr Hobbs has improved his health." Samuel Garth presents Mr. Hobbs, the surgeon, as Guâicum in *The Dispensary*, canto 6. Are these references to the surgeon who attended Mountfort?

said to me, you are now upon the brink of Eternity, and pray answer me truly, Who gave you this Wound, was it Mr. *Hill*, or my Lord *Mohun*?" Once more Mountfort answered, "*My Lord* Mohun *offered me no Violence, but whilst I was talking with my Lord* Mohun, Hill *struck me with his Left Hand, and with his Right Hand run me through, before I could put my Hand to my Sword.*" To William Hunt he made virtually the same remark and added, "*Hill was in me and was through me, before my Sword was out.*" Realizing that he had but a short time to live, he received the sacrament.[1]

Among the persons who were with Mountfort during his last hours were Ralph D'Avenant, the treasurer of the United Company, and Edward Porter,[2] who is remembered as a friend of Congreve's. When the actor's will was drawn up on a sheet of paper apparently torn from an account book, these two and William Hunt were witnesses. The document was brief:[3]

In the name of God Amen I William Mountfort of the parish of St Clement Danes in the County of Midd*lese*x Gentl^n (being of Sound Mind & Memory praysed be God) Doe make this my Last Will & Testament in manner following; I Give Devise & Bequeath All my Goods & P*e*rsonall Estate w^{t}soever and all such Debts Su$\overline{m}$s and Sums; of money w^{t}soever as are anywayes Due or payable to mee; unto my Deare Wife Susanna And make her Sole Executrix of this my will In trust for the payment of all my just Debts and ffunerall Charges and the Overplus I Give & Bequeath to my s^d Deare wife and to my Daughter Susanna &

1. *The Life and Times of Anthony Wood*, ed. Andrew Clark (Oxford, 1894), III, 411.

2. Several of Congreve's letters are addressed to Mr. Edward Porter "at his house in Surry street." In a letter to Joseph Keally dated June 26, 1706, Congreve writes, "I am removed to Mr. Porter's in Surry-street."

3. P.C.C. Fane 227.

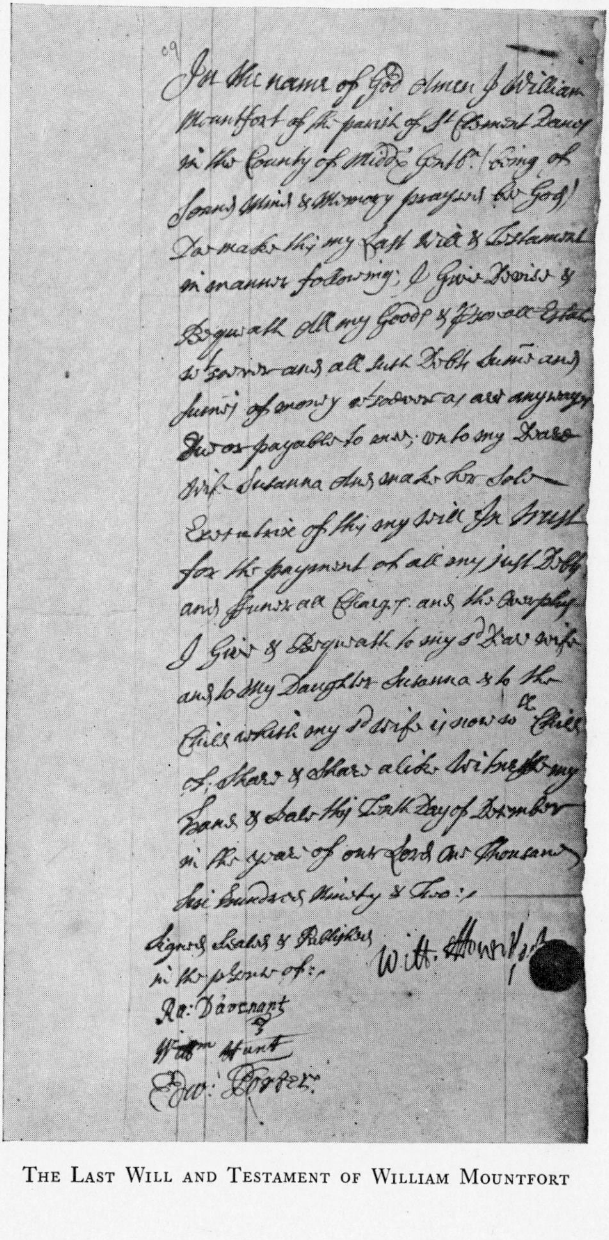

In the name of God Amen I William Mountfort of the parish of St Clement Danes in the County of Middx Gentl. (being of sound Mind & Memory praysed be God) Doe make this my Last Will & Testament in manner following; I Give Devise & Bequeath all my Goods & Personall Estate whatsoever and all such Debts summe and summs of money whatsoever as are anyways due or payable to mee; unto my Deare Wife Susanna And make her Sole Executrix of this my Will In trust for the payment of all my just Debts and Funerall Charges and the Overplus I Give & Bequeath to my sd Deare wife and to my Daughter Susanna & to the Child which my sd wife is now wth Child Share & Share alike Witness my hand & Seale this Tenth day of December in the yeare of our Lord One Thousand Six hundred Ninety & Two :/

Signed Sealed & Published in the presence of:/
Ra: Davenant
Wm Hunt
Edw: Porter

Will. Mountfort

The Last Will and Testament of William Mountfort

to the Child which my s^d wife is now wth Child of; Share & Share alike Witnesse my Hand & Seale this Tenth Day of December in the yeare of our Lord One Thousand Six Hundred Ninety & Two:/

It was signed "Will. Mountfort" in a shaky hand and sealed.

About one o'clock in the afternoon of Saturday, December 10, the sufferings of the dying man came to an end. Theatrical tradition tells us that the tragedy intended for presentation on that day was *Bussy D'Ambois*, in which Mountfort was to have acted the hero,[1] — a young man who meets his death through assassination, — and in which Mrs. Bracegirdle would doubtless, as usual, have appeared as his beloved Tamira.

IV

The news of the death of the actor spread rapidly, and the facts naturally became distorted. Robert Harley, when writing to Sir Edward Harley on December 10, reported inaccurately: "Last night, Lord Mohun, Captain Hill, and Mr. Knight having been hindered from attempting Mrs. Bracegirdle by Mr. Montford the actor, they dogged him, and at twelve at night killed him with three wounds. Lord Mohun was taken. The murder was at his own door in Norfolk Street." [2] On the same day, a letter to

1. The "Account" states: "But 'tis very remarkable, that the Night after he was kill'd he was to have Acted the Part of *Bussy D'Amboys*, in Mr. *Chapman*'s PLAY, bearing that Title; wherein he was to be shot through the Back in the Catastrophe, and his own Murder was accomplish'd by a Wound in that Part with a Sword; so that the same Tragedy, at least with very little Variation, was actually effected on himself, which he was only intended to represent on the THEATRE."

2. *Manuscripts of the Duke of Portland* (Historical Manuscripts Commission, 14th report, Appendix, Part II), III, 509.

Anthony à Wood stated: "Last night Mr. Mountford the player was kil'd by one capt. Clinton in some quarrel wherein the Lord Mohun had been concerned." [1] On the eleventh, Mr. Richard Lapthorne informed Mr. Richard Coffin: "yesterday the Lord Mohun fought with a player, and killed him." [2] On the thirteenth the Countess of Nottingham told her correspondent:

We have but little news here except of killing. That wretched creature my Lord Mohun, who is not sixteen years old tell April next, about a fortnight agoe was in a drunken quarrel wth my Lord Kennedy; on Friday night, wth one Hill about his one age, killed poore Montfort the player, and, as tis related, very barbarously.[3]

And Luttrell recorded, under date of December 10:

Last night lord Mohun, captain Hill of collonel Earles regiment, and others, pursued Mountfort the actor from the playhouse to his lodgings in Norfolk Street, where one kist him while Hill run him thro' the belly: they ran away, but his lordship was this morning seized and committed to prison. Mountfort died of his wounds this afternoon. The quarrell was about Bracegirdle the actresse, whom they would have trapan'd away, but Mountfort prevented it, wherefore they murthered him thus.

In this way misinformation grew: a Mr. Knight is concerned in the attempt; the men dogged Mountfort; the actor prevented the abduction; he was killed by a Captain Clinton; he was killed by Mohun.

On the day of Mountfort's death witnesses were sum-

1. *The Life and Times of Anthony Wood*, III, 411. "Hill" is used instead of "Clinton" in the text, but a footnote states that the name was "written at first 'capt . . . Clinton' but corrected to 'Hill,' a note being added 'Another letter saith, "by capt. . . . Hill".'"

2. *Fifth Report of the Royal Commission on Historical Manuscripts*, Appendix, p. 383.

3. *Correspondence of the Family of Hatton*, II, 187.

moned to appear before the justices at Hicks Hall. Among
these were the page, Thomas Lake, who had been arrested
during the night, and who was kept in prison for two days;
the surgeon John Bancroft, the neighbor John Warington;
Mrs. Dorothy Browne and her maid Ann Jones; Mrs. Anne
Bracegirdle and her maid Elizabeth Walker. If a manuscript preserved in the British Museum contains, as I believe, copies of the depositions made on this occasion,[1] the
others who gave evidence were Mrs. Martha Bracegirdle,
Gawen and Mrs. Mary Page, Hill's landlady Mrs. Ann
Rudd, the constable John Davenport, and the beadle William Merry. As a result of these hearings, Lord Mohun,
who was also examined, was bailed, his sureties being Lord
Gerard, Lady Mohun's uncle, and Mr. Charles Montague,
and the sum being two thousand pounds.[2]

Of those who appeared before the justices at Hicks Hall,
Elizabeth Walker was the only person openly to harbor a
grievance against the associates of the actor, although she
called Mountfort the "Friend [she] had most Respect for."
At the trial of Lord Mohun later, she was to allege that on
the morning of December 10 several of the players came
to her, asked her what she knew about the affair of the
night before, and then seemed displeased at what she had
to say. As they were leaving for Hicks Hall, they told her
they had no need of her evidence. But two or three hours
later she and her mistress were summoned. While she was
addressing the justices, Mrs. Bracegirdle stood before her
and said that the evidences confounded themselves. Another person remarked, "Hang her Jade, pull her by the
Coat."

1. See Appendix C.
2. Luttrell, II, 638; Forsythe, p. 41.

Because her evidence was displeasing, she was afraid to go home, and so she stayed with her sister during the remainder of the day. But about nine in the evening, she showed courage and returned to the house on Howard Street, where she found that all were "very inveterate" against her. Ann Jones, with whom she slept that night, gave her the unpleasing news that it was intended on Sunday to send for her to Mrs. Mountfort's in order to "rattle" her for the account she had given at Hicks Hall. When this information seemed to be confirmed the next morning by the appearance of a man sent by the actor's widow inquiring for her, she became frightened. Refusing to accompany him, she then demanded her wages from Mrs. Martha Bracegirdle and hurried from the house as soon as they were paid, despite the fact that she was urged to remain. When on Monday she examined her clothes, she discovered to her chagrin that she had left one of her aprons behind and had by mistake taken one belonging to her mistress. She went to her uncle, who was a porter, and asked him to return it for her. Then she learned that three bailiffs had been seeking her. Again frightened and fearing she might be sent to prison, she sought a justice of the peace and told him her story, but his only advice was for her to return to her mistress. Hearing also that she was wanted by the coroner's jury, she sent a neighbor to Mrs. Mountfort's to inform them that she was ready to wait upon them if they had not gone. In the meantime she remained at a nearby victualing house. The neighbor returned with the word from Mrs. Mountfort that they had done without her.

As a result of the coroner's inquest held on Monday, December 12, both Mohun and Hill were charged with murder. Luttrell notes that his lordship's mother "went to the king to interceed for her son, but was told 'twas a barbarous act, and that he would leave it to the law." He also reports, probably incorrectly as will be seen later, that following the findings at the inquest Mohun "was again taken up by a warrant from the lord cheife justice, and continues in custody."

On the night of Tuesday, the thirteenth, the unfortunate actor was laid to rest in the vault at St. Clement Danes. The funeral ceremonies were said to have been attended by a thousand persons, among whom were "a great many Gentlemen," who thus showed their respect "for one whom they Lov'd and Esteem'd." Royalty was not indifferent at the passing of the player, for the funeral anthem was sung by a group of choristers from Whitehall accompanied by Henry Purcell.[1] The great bell of the church, as it was ringing Mountfort's knell, cracked, a circumstance which was "taken much notice of by the criticks." [2]

Two days later, *The London Gazette* for December 12–15 contained the following advertisement, which was repeated in the issue of December 15–19:

Whereas it appears by an Inquisition taken before John Cowper *Esq., Chief Coroner of* Middlesex, *That Captain* Richard Hill, *did, on the 9th instant, about* 12 *at Night, in the Parish of St.* Clements Danes, *Murder Mr.* William Mountfort, *and that the said* Capt. Hill *immediately fled for the same: If any Persons can Apprehend him, or cause him to be Apprehended, they shall have* 20 l. *paid them by Mr.* Mountfort's *Widow, at her House in* Norfolk-street. *The said* Capt. Hill *is of a fair Complexion, then wore his own Hair, and is about* 18 *Years of Age.*[3]

1. Luttrell, II, 641; "Account."
2. *The Life and Times of Anthony Wood*, III, 411–412.
3. The issue of December 12–15 by mistake prints "*person*" instead of the

The plea of the widow and the reward offered were unsuccessful in bringing the murderer to justice. On January 19 Luttrell recorded the report that "capt. Hill (who kill'd Mr. Mountford) is taken in the Isle of Wight." Apparently this was a mistaken rumor, for nothing more is heard about the matter. Although the Lord Chief Justice Holt, on the strength of the coroner's inquest, had granted his warrant to apprehend Mohun,[1] the latter had evaded arrest. On January 11, however, he presented a petition to the House of Lords in which he alleges that since December 10, when the justices at Hicks Hall took his bail, a fresh warrant is out against him. To avoid "a chargeable imprisonment," he withdrew himself, but since he knows he is innocent, he is ready to surrender to the House. He prays that he may be granted a speedy trial, and in the meantime be admitted to bail.[2] The petition was referred to the Lord's Committee for Privileges.[3]

On January 13 Mohun surrendered himself to the House and was committed to the gentleman usher of the Black Rod, Sir Thomas Duppa.[4] On the following day the Marquis of Halifax reported from the Committee for Privileges that "they do not find any Precedent for a Peer's Trial at the Bar, but in *Westminster Hall*; and are of Opinion, That the Coroner's Inquest taken against him be sent for; and that, as to his desiring to be bailed, their Lordships think he ought to be committed to *The Tower of London*,

plural form and omits "*they*" before "*shall have* 20 l." These errors are corrected in the later issue.

1. Luttrell, II, 641.
2. *Manuscripts of the House of Lords, 1692–1693* (Historical Manuscripts Commission, 14th report, Appendix, Part VI), p. 294.
3. *Journals of the House of Lords*, XV, 179.
4. *Idem*, XV, 182.

and that as short a Time as may be thought convenient may be appointed for his Trial: That, the Lord *Mohun* having surrendered himself, an Order be made to discharge his Bail." These recommendations were carried out: the coroner's inquisition was read, his lordship was conveyed to the Tower by Sir Thomas Duppa, and the justices holding the sessions for the County of Middlesex were informed that the bail taken to assure his appearance was to be discharged as if he had appeared in person.[1]

The day of the trial was set for Tuesday, January 31. It was decided in the House that the prisoner was to have as counsel Sir Thomas Powis, Mr. Price, and Mr. Hawles; that the prosecutors on His Majesty's behalf were to be the king's counsel; that the clerk of the crown in Their Majesties Court of King's Bench and his deputy should attend; and that the lord high steward to be appointed by the king should be chosen speaker by the House for the days of the trial. All peers who were in town or within twenty miles of the town were summoned to attend upon pain of incurring the displeasure of the House, and no peer then in town might leave. Careful attention was also given to the physical arrangements. The scaffolding should be made strong; the box was to be reserved for foreign ministers; eleven benches in a favored situation were to be set aside for the guests of the lords, each of whom was to have not more than eight tickets of admission; another sort of ticket, which was to be at the disposal of the lord great chamberlain, would gain access to the other benches. Even thought was given to the traffic arrangements, for the steward of Westminster and his deputies were instructed to give strict orders "that no Carts nor Drays be suffered to pass to or fro in the

1. *Idem*, XV, 183, 184; British Museum Additional MS. 38855, fol. 137.

Streets, on *Tuesday* the One and Thirtieth Day of this
Instant *January*, between *Charing Cross* and *The Old
Palace Yard*, *Westminster*, between the Hours of Six of the
Clock in the Morning and Nine of the Clock at Night of
the same Day." [1]

V

On January 31 Thomas Osborne, Marquis of Carmarthen, who had been commissioned lord high steward,
appeared, so wrote Charles Hatton, with "y[e] largest and
finest coach and y[e] richest liveryes" that he had ever
seen.[2] In accordance with an earlier decision, the marquis
was unanimously chosen by his peers to be speaker for the
days of the trial. After considering various questions about
procedure, the members of the House of Lords present,
consisting of the Archbishop of Canterbury, fourteen
bishops, and eighty-five temporal peers, were ready to
adjourn into Westminster Hall, where the king and many
of the gentry and nobility of both sexes were awaiting
them.[3] At about twelve o'clock, accompanied by the
judges and the masters in chancery as well as by various
lesser officials, they, wearing their robes, entered the Hall
in which Richard II had been deposed, Charles I had been
condemned to death, and Cromwell had been installed as
lord protector.

The lords seated themselves upon the benches and the
Marquis of Carmarthen took his place upon the wool-pack.
With fitting ceremony he was presented with Their Majes-
ties' commission. Then the writ of certiorari directed to

1. *Journals of the House of Lords*, XV, 195, 196, 202, 206.
2. *Correspondence of the Family of Hatton*, II, 188.
3. Luttrell, III, 26.

the commissioners of oyer and terminer for the County of Middlesex to remove the indictment found before them against Lord Mohun, with the return and the record of the indictment, was read, and the lord high steward went to the chair placed upon "an Ascent just before the uppermost step of the Throne."

The deputy governor of the Tower brought Lord Mohun to the bar, "having the Ax carried before him by the Gentleman Jaylor of the *Tower*, who stood with it at the Bar, on the Right Hand of the Prisoner, turning the Edge from him." Since his voice could not be heard at such a distance, the steward asked and was granted permission to return to the wool-pack. In his brief address to the prisoner, he expressed the hope that the youthful peer could not so early have had his hands in blood, reminded him that he had the good fortune to be tried in full parliament, and assured him that he had nothing to fear except his guilt. If there was room for any abatement of severity, he might reasonably expect it from their lordships. At the same time Mohun should not flatter himself that any favor would be shown "beyond what Honour and Justice can allow."

The clerk of the crown read the indictment, which charged Mohun and Hill with "*feloniously*, *wilfully*, *and of* . . . *Malice afore-thought*" killing and murdering William Mountfort. In opening the case, the attorney-general, Sir John Somers, urged:

it is not insisted upon, that the Noble Lord at the Bar gave the Mortal Stroak with his own Hand; Nor is it alledged in the Indictment: The Indictment findeth the Wound to have been given by the Hand of *Richard Hill*; but if my Lord the Prisoner was of his Party, if he Concurr'd with him in the Thing, if he was Present and Abetting to the Fact, though he did not strike a stroke, though he was no more than a looker on, when the thing was done, the Law saith, he is a Principal in the Murder.

Whether my Lords Case will fall within this Rule, is the Point for your Lordships to Determine, when the Witnesses are heard.

Before the witnesses were summoned, it was necessary to clear a space into which the crowd had pressed forward at the bar between the prisoner and the king's counsel. Those who were called to give evidence under oath on behalf of Their Majesties against the prisoner were John Hodgson, George Powell, Mrs. Knight, Mrs. Elizabeth Sandys, John Rogers, William Dixon, Mrs. Anne Bracegirdle, Gawen Page, Mrs. Mary Page, Mrs. Dorothy Browne, Richard Row, William Merry, Thomas Fennel, James Bassit, Mrs. Brewer, John Davenport, John Bancroft, and William Hunt. Charles Knowles, who was summoned several times, did not appear.[1]

Then Lord Mohun examined his witnesses, who were not under oath: Mr. Brereton, Thomas Lake, Mrs. Elizabeth Walker, Mrs. Ann Jones, Edward (or John) Warington, and Mrs. Ann Knevitt. The boy Thomas Lake spoke in so inaudible a voice that one of the court officers had to repeat his testimony, which the attorney-general contended differed from what was contained in the deposition he had made before the coroner. Elizabeth Walker, the maid who

1. The journals of the House of Lords for January 20 and 28, 1693, contain orders that certain persons attend the trial as witnesses. Those who were thus summoned, but who did not give evidence, were Samuell Bucke, Esq., Thomas Owen, Esq., John Herbert, Esq., Anne Rudd, James Jerwyn, Michaell Lee, Martha Bracegirdle, Hamlet Bracegirdle, William Nuthall, Thomas Hildrop, Mary Harbyn, William Sprigg, Ellen Feasye, Elizabeth Jackson, John Sea-grave, and Anne Knight. The witnesses at the trial, whose names do not appear in the journals among those ordered to attend, were Mrs. Frances Maria Knight, Mrs. Brewer, John Rogers, William Dixon, William Hunt, and Mr. Brereton.

had left Mrs. Bracegirdle's service because she was afraid
of being "rattled" by Mrs. Mountfort, and who had succeeded in concealing herself from the attorney-general
until the trial, also spoke in a low voice, but she was more
willing to talk than the boy. At one time she became
muddled in her speech and caused great laughter to the
spectators by saying, when referring to Mountfort and
Hill: "I saw them Fighting, making passes at one another,
I saw them Engaged, I never saw men naked Fighting so
in my Life." There was such confusion in the hall while
she and Ann Knevitt were giving their evidence that the
lord high steward instructed the crier to call for silence and
the lord great chamberlain, the Earl of Lindsay, to take
some order with the people, who "cannot hear themselves
what the Witnesses say, and therefore . . . are Resolved
[the peers] shall not hear them neither." After Mohun's
witnesses had made their statements, Thomas Lake was
again called to hear read the deposition that had been
taken before the coroner on December 12.[1] Mrs. Bracegirdle was also questioned about her servant, and the loquacious Elizabeth Walker once more aired her grievances
against actors. She was afraid to go to Mrs. Mountfort's
on the Sunday following the murder because "Players
have a worse Reputation than other People."

In a few sentences Mohun summarized the deductions
to be drawn from the evidence submitted by his witnesses
and then concluded by redeclaring his innocence. He was

---

1. His sworn statement before the coroner was: "*Mr.* Hill *said, he was able to
vindicate himself, and bid Mr. Mountford to draw, and they both pushed at each
other with their Swords, and my Lord said he would stand by his Friend, and Mr.
Hill was his Friend.*" Upon questioning at the trial by the attorney-general,
Lake said, "my Lord said, he would not go, he would stay by his Friend, for
Mr. *Hill* was his Friend."

followed by the solicitor-general, Sir Thomas Trevor, whose duty it was to repeat the evidence presented on behalf of the king. In the midst of his discourse, a lady fell into a fit in one of the galleries, and thus occasioned an interruption of about a quarter of an hour until she was removed. After summarizing the evidence, he declared that it was plain there was a premeditated malice in Hill, "by his own Declarations preceding, by what was done at the time of the Fact committed, and by Stabbing him before his Sword was drawn." The question which the lords would have to decide was whether Mohun was privy to Hill's design, "and did so far agree in it, as to keep him Company to Assist and Incourage him. For if he was Privy, and knew of *Hills* Design, and stayed there for that purpose, to give him Assistance in it, . . . he will be as much Guilty of the Murther, as *Hill* that actually killed him." And in conclusion the solicitor-general made this appeal to the peers:

I know you very well remember, and will carefully Recollect all the Evidence, both for the King and for the Prisoner, and your Lordships will consider that it is a Case of Blood, and if your Lordships think him Guilty, tho' he be one of your own Body, you will adjudge him so, if not, you will acquit him; and therefore I leave the matter to your Lordships just Determination.

The peers then signified their pleasure to adjourn to their own House; whereupon they departed in the same order as that in which they had entered Westminster Hall. The king had withdrawn and left for Kensington earlier in the afternoon. In their House, the lords spiritual were granted permission to be absent for the remainder of the trial; and four temporal peers who had been present at the proceedings in Westminster Hall but who did not return to the House, were fined one hundred pounds each to be distributed among the poor of the parishes in Westminster. It was also ordered that any peer who was present on the opening day of the trial but who should be absent on the morrow should be committed to the Tower. Mohun was then remanded prisoner to the Tower with the order that he be brought to the bar in Westminster Hall on the morrow.[1]

Although the prisoner, the judges, the counsel, and the witnesses were in attendance at the Hall on Wednesday, February 1, the lords remained in their House all that day debating on the evidence until they finally adjourned about eight o'clock. Since Thursday was Candlemas Day, they did not return to the business until Friday. After additional debating the peers near four o'clock in the afternoon again marched in procession to the court at Westminster Hall and presented to the judges and counsel hypothetical questions, the answers to which might determine them in deciding about the guilt of Lord Mohun. In each instance the counsel for the prisoner stated their opinions and then the judges gave theirs. The counsel for the king had nothing to say concerning any of the seven questions, for they felt it inconsistent with their duty to enter into a debate upon supposed cases.

The first three questions were answered in the same manner by both the counsel for the prisoner and the judges. Objection was raised to the fourth by John Sheffield, Earl of Mulgrave, and so the lords adjourned to their House to consider it. After a debate of about an hour, they returned to Westminster Hall, the question was again proposed, and once more counsel and judges agreed as to the answer.

1. *Journals of the House of Lords*, XV, 209–210.

The fifth question, proposed by Daniel Finch, Earl of Nottingham, however, did not bring forth unanimity of opinion:

Whether a Person knowing of the design of another to lie in wait to Assault a third Man, and accompanying him in that design, if it shall happen that the third Person be killed at that time in the presence of him who knew of that design, and accompanied the other in it, be Guilty in Law of the same Crime with the Party who had that design and killed him, though he had no actual hand in his Death?

The counsel for Mohun argued that it would not be murder because "to make any thing Murder there must be pre-pensed malice in the person that is to be found Guilty of it, or some precedent Agreement to do it, or some Act of Aiding or Assisting of the Person who doth it; but as this Case is, here is nothing of Malice doth appear, or that the Person who accompanied the other in his Design had any sort of Malice against the Person Assaulted." The judges, on the other hand, agreed that it would be murder on the part of the accompanying person: "For he being ac-quainted with the Design, and knowing of the Intention of the Party to Commit Murder, or do an unlawful Act, upon which Death might ensue, accompanying him in that Design, he shews an Approbation of it, and gives him greater Courage to put it in Execution." As his vote was later to show, the opinion of the judges had greater weight with Nottingham than that of Mohun's counsel.

The sixth question also did not prove easy to answer:

If a Person be by, named William, when Thomas said, He would stab John, upon which William said, He would stand by his Friend; and afterwards Thomas doth actually murder John, and William

is present at the same Murder: Whether the Law will make William
equally guilty with Thomas, *or what Crime* William *is guilty of?*

Two of the prisoner's counsel and one of the judges agreed
that William, in the case as stated, would be guilty of
murder. The others were inclined to affirm that William's
saying he would stand by his friend indicated a willingness
to assist him in the murder, but they also contended that
it would be necessary to determine by means of the evidence whether he was present, at the time of the crime, for
that purpose or not.

The seventh question being disposed of quickly, the
lords returned to their House.

On the next day, Saturday, February 4, the peers, after
debating on the evidence, filed into Westminster Hall
about four o'clock in the afternoon, prepared to give their
verdict. To the question *"Whether my Lord* Mohun *be
Guilty of the Murder of* William Mountford, *whereof he
stands Indicted, or Not Guilty?"* each peer, beginning with
the youngest baron, Lord Lemster, and ending with the
lord high steward, the Marquis of Carmarthen, stood up
in his place uncovered, laid his right hand on his breast,
and pronounced his judgment. After the eighty-three
lords present had thus voiced their decisions, the lord high
steward announced, "My Lords, I have carefully taken
all your Lordships Opinions, and find the Numbers to be
thus: My Lords that have found my Lord *Mohun* to be
Guilty are Fourteen; my Lords that have found him Not
Guilty are Sixty nine." [1] The prisoner was then brought

1. The fourteen who considered Mohun guilty were Lords Capell, Clifford of
Lansborough, and Colpeper, Viscount Weymouth, the Earls of Warrington,
Monmouth, Portland, Rochester, Nottingham, Sandwich, Kingston, Westmor-
land, Bridgewater, and Oxford. Among those who voted "Not Guilty" were

to the bar by the chief governor of the Tower and discharged. Then the clerk of the crown proclaimed that the lord high steward intended to dissolve his commission; whereupon Carmarthen took the white staff in both his hands and broke it in two. The trial being at an end, the peers adjourned to their House and completed the business by releasing from paying the fines the four lords who had absented themselves on Tuesday.[1]

The verdict was not entirely unexpected. On the first day of the trial, Charles Hatton wrote in a letter: "ye generall opinion is my Ld Mohun will be acquitted";[2] and Luttrell recorded the same belief in his journal. But the decision of the peers was not accepted without dissent. Queen Mary, in commenting on general conditions, wrote,

twas impossible not to be extremely melancoly and discouraged. And when I considerd the condition of the nation, I was no less so. So universal a corruption (: the whole nobility giving such a proof of it in their behaviour at Lord Mohuns tryal) that we seem only prepard for vengeance.[3]

Evelyn noted in his diary on February 4:

After five days trial and extraordinary contest, the Lord Mohun was acquitted by the Lords of the murder of Montford the Player, notwithstanding the Judges, from the pregnant witnesses of the fact, had declar'd him guilty; but whether in commiseration of his youth, being not 18 years old, tho' exceeding dissolute or upon whatever other reason, the K. himselfe present

---

the Earls of Dorset, Devon, Lindsay, and Pembroke, the Lord Marquis of Halifax, the Dukes of St. Albans, Northumberland, Ormonde, Somerset, and Norfolk, and the lord high steward, the Marquis of Carmarthen.

1. *Journals of the House of Lords*, XV, 214.
2. *Correspondence of the Family of Hatton*, II, 189.
3. R. Doebner, *Memoirs of Mary Queen of England* (London, 1886), p. 59.

some part of the trial, and satisfied, as they report, that he was culpable, 69 acquitted him, only 14 condemned him.

And on the same day, Robert Harley in writing to Sir Edward Harley could but report:

This day, the town having clamoured at the delay, gave judgment of not guilty. They have taken a news writer into custody for saying the evidence was strong enough to hang a commoner.[1]

From the evidence adduced at the trial and the legal opinion presented, the verdict seems perfectly fair. Hill alone was guilty. In love with Mrs. Bracegirdle, who was indifferent towards him, and believing that Mountfort was her successful lover or had, in some way, prejudiced her against him, he had several times openly expressed his desire to be the death of the actor. When the attempt at abduction — of which I believe that Hamlet Bracegirdle and Elizabeth Walker had prior knowledge as well as Mohun — failed, Hill accompanied the actress to her door. There he insisted upon waiting until she appeared in order that he might beg her pardon, with the idea possibly, when her anger had cooled, of again pressing his claims to her affection. As a means of passing the time, he and his comrade, both of whom had been tippling at the White Horse and the Horseshoe taverns earlier in the evening, sent for a bottle of wine which they consumed in the street. Then Mountfort appeared, and after he had made a slighting remark to Mohun concerning Hill, the latter, who had been heated by the drink and whose hatred for his supposed rival was simmering, struck the actor a blow on the ear and gave him his death-wound before he had an opportunity to defend himself.

1. *Manuscripts of the Duke of Portland*, III, 513.

Mohun's part in the affair was passive. A young man about town with plenty of time on his hands, he was ready to accompany his friend on his adventure, and, once he had started, he determined to see it through. During the attempted abduction he appears to have remained in the coach, although he declared to Mrs. Browne that he had saved Mrs. Bracegirdle from the mob. These words may have been merely a bit of empty boasting. When the watch approached, he offered to surrender his sword. There is no indication that he held Mountfort in conversation in order that Hill might have an opportunity to stab him. Knowing that he was guiltless and also possibly feeling weakened because of the wound of two days before, he made no effort to accompany his friend as he ran up Surrey Street. His high-sounding remarks to the constable at the Round House may be considered a display of bravado.

It is of course possible, but no absolutely conclusive evidence was brought forth to prove it, that the two men waited in Howard Street with the determination of causing the actor's death. It is, on the other hand, just as proper to believe that Hill's sole purpose in remaining was his desire to speak to Mrs. Bracegirdle. Although on various occasions he had threatened to be the death of Mountfort, his act at the moment, I think, was impulsive, and his companion was therefore not guilty of complicity. The House of Lords, on the facts presented, could do nothing less than acquit Mohun of the charge of murder.[1]

1. The Earl of Birkenhead in *Famous Trials of History*, p. 88, feels, after a careful study of the evidence, that the acquittal of Mohun was right. It was a case of suspicion. "It is highly probable that there was no design against Mountford, that the meeting was by chance and that Hill acted without premeditation. It was an affair of seconds, and unless Lord Mohun realised what was toward, and aided and abetted the murderer, then whatever crime he had committed that night he was guiltless of murder." See also Forsythe, pp. 32–35.

A Tragical SONG:
OR,
Mr. Wil. Montfort,

The Famous Actor Unfortunately Kill'd.

Ture of *Mary Live Long.*

GOod People draw near,
  And hear my sad Ditty
With Hearts full of Pity,
  This Tragical Year
Is bloudy indeed ;
  Some they fairly do fight,
Others ftab'd in the Night,
  as they do go home,
Brave *Montfort* the Player,
B ave *Montfort* the Player,
He lately was one.

His Name ftill will laft
  In Court Town or Country,
By Cits, or the Gentry,
  Till Ages are paft
For Acts on the ftage ;
  For in playing a Part,
He excells the fam'd *Hart*,
  Or *Moon* that's dead too,
Nay, no one thats livi-g,
Nay, no one thats living,
Can *Montfort* out-do.

His Carriage was fuch,
  In all Converfation,
To be free from Paffion,
  And never thought much
To oblige any one ;
  From a Lord to a Cit,
He was free with his VVit,
  And Courteous withal :
But now alas Killing,
But now alas Killing,
Is us'd all in all.

Each one does lament
  His death, fince life s fhortn'd
By b'oudy misfortune,
  And cries out a main
Poor *Montfort* is gone,
  It is all ore the Town,
VVas the like ever known,
  To ufe a man fo,
When coming to's Lodging,
When coming to's Lodging,
He fhould be run through.

O cruel hard Fate,
  Since *Murder's* in fafhion,
VVith the Englifh Nation,
  That men cannot fcape,
Being kill'd by the Sword;
  One can hardly pafs by,
But another does cry,
  Lets kill the next man.
Some never will leave it,
Some never will leave it,
Untill they be hang'd.

Here's *Montfort* of late,
  Tho young and beloved,
How foon Life is moved,
  VVhen malice or hate
Shall once refolve Death,
  As he went without Light,
He was run *thro* that Night,
  And dy'd the next day ;
So he thats *Moon*-blinded,
So he thats *Moon* blinded
  May foon lofe his way.

London, *Printed for* Charles Barnes.

A SONG ON THE DEATH OF MOUNTFORT

VI

Apparently the first literary effusion to result from the death of Mountfort was some halting verses by an unknown writer. Intended to be sung to the tune of *Mary Live Long*, they were printed on a single sheet with black border and had as title, "A Tragical Song: or, Mr. Wil. Montfort, The Famous Actor Unfortunately Kill'd." As poetry, they are beneath criticism, but they have interest because of their praise of Mountfort as an actor who excelled Charles Hart and who was unsurpassed by any living player. His wit was not forgotten, nor was the opportunity for a pun on the name of Mohun (pronounced *Moon*) overlooked in the final stanza. A reproduction of the song appears on the opposite page.[1]

Near the time of the trial, the prolific hack-writer Tom Brown was ready with six stanzas entitled "*The Ladies Lamentation for their* Adonis: *Or, an* ELEGY *on the Death of Mr.* Mountford *the Player*." In these verses, which could be sung to the tune of *Packington's Pound*, were stressed the fondness of the female sex for the actor, his pleasing appearance, his ability as singer and dancer, and the fact that he — a "base and unmannerly *Whig*" — had once spoken disrespectfully of King James.[2]

---

1. Reproduced by permission of the Huntington Library, San Marino, California. The song was kindly brought to my attention by Miss Lucyle Hook. The "*Moon*" mentioned in the second stanza is Michael Mohun, the actor.

2. The text quoted is found on pp. 235–237 in *The Remains of Mr. Tho. Brown, Serious and Comical, in Prose and Verse* (London, 1720). With some verbal changes, it appears in MS. Egerton 2623, fol. 50, as "Elegy on Mumford. To the Tune of Packington's Pound." For the tune see William Chappell, *Old English Popular Music* (London, 1893), I, 259–260.

I

Poor *Mountford* is gone, and the Ladies do all
Break their Hearts for this *Beau*, as they did for *D'Val*,
And they the two Brats for this Tragedy damn,
At *Kensington*-Court, and the Court of *Bantam*.
    They all vow and swear,
    That if any Peer
Shou'd acquit the young Lord, he shou'd pay very dear;
Nor will they be pleas'd with him, who on Throne is,
If he do's not his Part, to revenge their *Adonis*.

II

With the Widow, their amorous Bowels do yearn;
There are divers pretend to an equal Concern;
And, by her Persuasion, their Hearts they reveal,
In case of *not guilty* to bring an Appeal.
    They all will unite,
    The young Blades to indite,
And in Prosecution will joyn Day and Night;
In the mean while, full many a Tear and Groan is,
Where'er they meet, for their departed *Adonis*.

III

With the Ladies foul Murder's a horrible Sin,
Of one handsome without, tho' a Coxcomb within;
For not being a *Beau*, the sad Fate of poor *Crab*,
Tho' himself hang'd for Love, was a Jest to each Drab:
    Then may *Jer'my* live long,
    And may *Risby* among
The Fair, with *Jack Barkley*, and *Culpeper* throng;
May no Ruffian, whose Heart as hard as a Stone is,
Kill any of these for a Brother *Adonis*.

IV

No Lady henceforth can be safe with her *Beau*,
They think, if this Slaughter unpunish'd shou'd go;
Their Gallants, for whose Persons they most are in Pain,
Must no sooner be envy'd, but strait must be slain.
    For all *Bracegirdle*'s Shape,
    None car'd for the Rape,

Nor whether the Virtuous their Lust did escape,
Their Trouble of Mind, and their Anguish alone, is
For the too sudden Fate of departed *Adonis*.

V

Let not ev'ry vain Spark think that he can engage
The Heart of a Female, like one on the Stage;
His Face, and his Voice, and his Dancing, are rare,
And wherever they meet they prevail with the Fair:
      But no Quality Top,
      Charms like Mr. *Hop*,
Adorn'd on the Stage, and in *East-India* Shop;
So that each from Miss *Felton*, to ancient *Drake Jone* is
Bemoaning the Death of the Player *Adonis*.

VI

Yet *Adonis* in spight of this new Abjuration,
Did banter the lawful King of this great Nation;
Who call'd *God's Anointed* a foolish old Prig,
Was both a base and unmannerly *Whig*;
      But since he is dead,
      No more shall be said,
For he in Repentance has laid down his Head;
So I wish each Lady, who in mournful Tone is,
In Charity grieve for the Death of *Adonis*.

The murder and trial also called forth a more ambitious effort, *The Player's Tragedy. Or, Fatal Love, A New Novel*, printed in 1693 and sold by Randal Taylor.[1] The author naturally did not wish to have his name known, and so he refrained from signing the dedicatory epistle addressed to James Wilson. In the introduction, after commenting on how actors were held in great esteem by the ancient Romans, he goes on to say,

But if Custom has now render'd the Familiarity and Conversation of Players *more scandalous to the precise in the decorums of*

1. It is interesting to note that Randal Taylor also sold *The Successfull Straingers, King Edward the Third*, and *Greenwich Park*, as well as *The Tryal of Charles Lord Mohun*.

Quality, and Vertue, than of Old; yet Love, *that mighty* Leveller, *has kept up their esteem among the Amorous of both Sexes; the* Ladies, *and the* Cavaliers, *since the Glorious restoration of the* Theatre, *meeting with more agreeable Objects on the Stage, than in the Boxes, or the Pit, the Parks, or the Drawing-Room.*

He hopes to gratify "*the Young and the Gay of both Sexes, in Presenting them with this following Narrative.*" He feels confident that "*they can't think the Subject unworthy their perusal, since they think themselves the most happy in the affections of* Nymphs *and* Hero's *of the* Theatre, *the two Chief of which compose* [*their*] *present Entertainment.*" He also begs the critical reader's pardon, if he runs not to the "*Head and Original of the* Heroine *of* [*his*] *History,*" since — to quote his words exactly —:

I have two Reasons that deter me from it: First, the uncertainty I should be involv'd in, which might make me derogate from them I ought to Magnifie. Next, because I propose only one Great Action *as my aim; to which, all I have to say is conducive. 'Tis the* Fatal End *of their* Amours, *not their* Lives, *that I here pretend to attempt in this* Novel, *having furnish'd my self with the best Information I could get, to render it perfect, and satisfactory.*

The principal figures in the Mountfort tragedy are presented in but a slightly veiled manner. Mrs. Bracegirdle becomes Bracilla; Mountfort, Monfredo; Hill, Montano; and Lord Mohun, Count de la Lune. Since *The Player's Tragedy* is a volume of great rarity, it seems proper to give a rather complete résumé of its contents and to quote directly the most pertinent passages. It begins as follows:

Bracilla the Young, and the Charming, that had grown up on the Stage, amidst the perpetual Addresses of her Admirers, and yet seem'd insensible of all the Efforts of Love, as if Heaven had given her Charms to enflame the Heart, without any Compassion

to Redress those Miseries her Eyes daily caused to all that beheld her, is believ'd at last, to have found all her cold indifference
melt at the secret and well-mannag'd Advances of *Monfredo*'s
Love.

How happy she made him in private I shall not dare to Divine; yet the Publick Favours she bestow'd, discover'd she cou'd
ill conceal the Passion she had entertain'd for him, in whom a
Wife had so Powerful a Claim. Nor could he better dissemble
his affection on all occasions, espousing her Interest and Affairs
with a Zeal and Concern beyond the Engagements of a bare and
unbias'd Friendship; which neither had, nor hop'd a more near
and close Obligation.

If *Bracilla* was deaf before to all those who were dying at her
feet for *Love*, she now grew even rude, and uncivil, especially in
Monfredo's presence, in which there seem'd to be an aw upon
her Actions, for fear of provoking the Jealousie or neglect of a
Lover she valu'd. Whether this were the true Cause of this or
no, I'll not pretend to determine; but this I'm sure was esteem'd
so, not only by those whom their Love of her had made narrow
Observers of her Actions, but also by others, to whom both her
and her Actions were as indifferent as their mutual indiscretion
would permit.

This discovery of the happy Rival, that made all her other
Adorers sigh in vain, created *Monfredo* a great many Enemies,
and those of the most dangerous kind, Despairing and Neglected
Lovers, who cou'd not but be provok'd to see him bear off that
Prize from them, for which, as a Marry'd Man, he seem'd so
very ill qualified.

I must confess how much Marriage may unqualifie a Man to
the Pretensions to the Ladies, I know not, but for all things else
there never was a Man better made for success with them; for
he was Handsom, cou'd Sing, Dance, and Play on the Musick,
had a Manly presence, and yet a soft Effeminacy in his face,
that cou'd not but render him agreeable to the wanton dalliances
of the Fair. The Play-House had furnish'd him with a smatter-
ing in Poetry, and a qualification much more taking with his
Female, as well as Male Acquaintance; a forward and bold
Assurance, both in Love, and Conversation; he knew his whole

stock of Wit, and valu'd it to the heighth, and always set it off
to its greatest advantage. He had the Reputation of Writing
three or four Plays, and therefore 'tis no wonder he carry'd
Bracilla from all the *Poets*, and her other Admirers, since he
pleaded in a double capacity, as *Player*, and *Poet* too. So that it
was no easie matter for any one to gain the Fort he had won, and
Garrison'd so well; and the *Poets*, whose *Love* and *Perseverance*
are as volatile as their Wits, soon gave over the Siege; but the
Unfortunate *Montano* was too far engag'd to have it in his power
to retreat, tho' he saw with how unequal a force he contended,
yet Love fixt him before her, and he hop'd all the Batteries he
had rais'd of Sighs and Vows, and a constant attack of daily
attendance, and officiousness, wou'd at last win the most im-
pregnable Fortress.

Montano indeed had the advantage of Merit, but that is never
regarded by Womankind; was a Gentleman, young, and gay,
and who offer'd her a Heart entire, and never acquainted with
any Love but hers; whilst *Monfredo*, had been lavish of his stock
of Love for several years, had dy'd at the feet of not a few, and
given away himself, by all the Oaths and Vows of perpetual
Adoration of a protesting Lover, to more than her. *Montano* had
not yet seen Ninteen, and was now perishing in the bloom of his
Youth for her, whereas *Monfredo* had pass'd above Thirty
Years, and by the several changes of his Affections, had discover'd, that his Heart wou'd never break for Love; yet *Montano*
sigh'd in vain, with all his Youth and Passion, whilst *Monfredo*
was happy with less desert.

With indignation our young Souldier (for *Montano* was a
Captain in the *Gensdarm's* of the Houshold) saw himself out-
rival'd by a *Player*, and wou'd often have attack'd him as a
Souldier ought, had not his Honour curb'd his Passion, by re-
membring him 'twas below him to use him so much like a Gentleman. This made him for a great while forbear all other Resentment, than the justest and highest contempt of him, still
pursuing the flying *Bracilla* with all the assiduity and fire of
Love. Each day he came to her to seek a cure for those Wounds
she had made in his tender Bosome, and each day he enlarg'd
'em, by beholding the relentless cause of all his sufferings; which

were now arriv'd to that heighth, that he was neither able to bear 'em, nor yet knew how to remove them.

Montano then sought out a noble youth, the Count de la Lune, and laid "open his wounded Bosome to him." That evening the two friends went to a tavern adjoining the theatre accompanied by Gerardo, "an old experienc'd Souldier in the Wars of *Love*." Upon learning of Montano's passion and upon hearing from the Count that Bracilla had "nothing taking but her Youth, and affected Coyness," Gerardo remarked that this coyness was not due to "her Vertue," but to "her Constancy in Love, *Monfredo* having taken Possession of her heart." Montano then related how he had often seen her act without much regard to her beauty or person, until about a year ago when he and the Count, after drinking, went behind the scenes.

Bracilla happen'd to Act that Night, the Wife of an *Unhappy Favourite*, and look'd so Charming in the Expression, of all the Innocence and Passion, her part requir'd, that whilst she well represented *Love* without any, she fir'd my Heart with a real, and not yet extinguish'd flame.

With difficulty, the Count persuaded him to withdraw and plied him so with liquor that before morning Montano forgot "not only *Bracilla*, but all things else; till Sleep restor'd [him] next day, both [his] memory and pain." When he again went to the theatre, Bracilla acted "in Man's Cloaths, a fond pretty innocent Lover" and his ruin was completed. He walked behind the scenes at the first opportunity, but she would not listen to his protestations. He asked if she was indeed "so very irreconcilable an Enemy to Love." She replied, "Why, Sir, shou'd you doubt it? Do you expect to find that on the Stage? We represent too many of its follies to be guilty of them our selves."

After the play, in melancholy mood, he proceeded to his lodgings, wrote some verses on his departure from her, and again passed a sleepless night. He continued to attend the playhouse every time Bracilla acted. He had not noticed that she showed any great aversion to him until recently, when she began to avoid him and to be uncivil, "especially if *Monfredo* were present, or in the House." Undaunted by her indifference to his letters, he invited her and some of her friends to a collation on her birthday, but she did not come. He thereupon had the serenade which he had prepared sung under her window. But all was in vain.

nor could I possibly Divine the Cause of it, 'till some of the Actors whisper'd about some suspicions of *Monfredo*'s greatness with her, and his immeasurable Zeal for her Interest, to ev'n injustice to others of the House; he wou'd not willingly let any one remain in the House, that gave any cause to suspect that she wou'd come into Competition with *Bracilla* in Excellence of Acting, and as one of the Players inform'd me, on this account, under pretence of easing the House of unnecessary Charge, prevail'd with the Masters, to dismiss *Rogera* [1] who was a very promising Actress, tho' he was oblig'd to re-admit her afterwards, to make way for the Sister of a Boy that waited much on *Bracilla*, and supply'd the Place of a Lackey.

He became jealous of Monfredo, and thought at various times of ridding himself of this rival, but then he considered it would be a blemish to his honor to fight a fellow of the actor's station. Frequently he dogged "*Monfredo*, his Wife and *Bracilla*" home from the theatre. He took

1. Probably Mrs. Rogers, whose first recorded rôle was that of Teresia in Shadwell's *The Volunteers* (presented late in November or in December, 1692). She retired from acting in 1719.

notice that they would part at her lodgings, but some time afterwards she would leave for a house "a pretty way from her home" and about a quarter of an hour later Monfredo would meet her there. After watching these proceedings many times, Montano wrote her letters referring to these nocturnal trysts. She resented the action, and the next time they met she told him that she would be forced to vindicate her reputation by law if he continued to asperse her. He made the best apology possible, and she left him with more civility than formerly. His passion increased. Although words often passed between Monfredo and him, he did not seek a quarrel because there was a certainty of their being parted.

The worldly-wise Gerardo, after hearing the lover's tale, told Montano that he had pursued a wrong method with the actress, who was not to be moved by those generous principles which might win persons of education and honor. Instead, he must make use of money and the services of a bawd. Gerardo then brought Coromella to them from the pit of the nearby playhouse. After providing her with an excellent repast, the men broached the subject. She regaled them with a long tale of how she served a count who loved a certain Clelia, and afterwards promised to bring Bracilla to Montano on the following night.

But Coromella wished to help this same Clelia, who had fallen in love with Montano, having observed him from a side-box, and so she told that lady that she must impersonate Bracilla. She also purchased a pair of gloves exactly similar to those the actress was to wear, and instructed Montano to give them to his mistress and to note that she will wear them on the morrow in the play. Accordingly at night Montano visited Clelia, thinking her the actress. The next day at the theatre he saw the gloves on Bracilla's hands and noticed more charms in her face than he had ever observed before. He was enraptured. After several similar interviews he discovered the truth and in anger swore revenge on Coromella. But after Clelia begged to keep the gloves for his dear sake and wished that Bracilla loved him more than she, he begged her pardon for his rudeness and left.

At the theatre the actress appeared more charming than ever. Coromella sent him a letter, saying she would put him into possession of Bracilla's person if he would not be angry and telling him where he might find her unattended the next day.

The Lover was at the place with his Coach before the appointed Hour, and soon saw *Bracilla* coming all alone towards it; as soon as she came near him, he jump'd out of the Coach, and caught her in his Arms, and bore her away into the Coach, strugling, and screaming; the Coachman soon fasten'd up the Door, and began to drive away as if the Devil were in him, but by her Screams which he in vain endeavours to stop with his Kisses; the Mobb took the Alarm, and soon stop'd the Coach, and deliver'd the distressed Damsel from him, and he with some difficulty made his escape from them.

After this rebuff he sought out the Count and Gerardo and told them of his misfortunes. The suggestions made by these two did not seem satisfactory to Montano, who felt that Monfredo possessed her very soul and that she would not run the risk of offending him.

At this point the author of the novel apparently became tired of his task, for he soon brought his work to an end with an abrupt conclusion:

That Lett methinks (*said Gerardo*) should be easily removed, if he be so sawcy and insolent as they say he is, and if he will,

being the Property of another, interlope in the free Trade, he
ought to be punished, or put out of the way a while till you succeed in your Wishes.

The Company after a little time, broke up, and the Count and
Montano were together toward *Bracilla*'s Lodgings, contriving
how they should get in to her, and whilst they were walking
thereabouts, *Monfredo* came by, and meeting the Count, a little
too familiar, begins to Catechise him, and to speak against his
Conversation with *Montano*, who he little thought so near. The
Place and Language his Rival us'd, concurring with the Vehe-
mence of his disappointed Passion, he drew, and in the Encounter ran *Monfredo* through: He made his Escape, but the
Count was taken, and upon a Tryal for the Fact, is clear'd of it
by vast odds of his Peers, *Monfredo* Dying the next Day.
Montano in a little time got safe out of the Nation, but whether
this fatal Love expir'd with this Tragedy or no, I am to seek.

It is impossible to say nearly two centuries and a half
after the event whether there was any truth in Hill's belief
that Mountfort was a lover of Mrs. Bracegirdle. That the
names of the two were linked by gossip is clear not only
from the captain's words as reported at the trial but from
The Player's Tragedy with its account of the "*Fatal End of
their Amours*." Some years later Tom Brown returned to
the subject in one of his fluent and scurrilous *Letters from
the Dead to the Living*. Here Bully Dawson describes to
Bully W—— how he has met "*Mumford* the Player, looking as Pale as a Ghost, sailing forward as gently as a
Catterpiller cross a Sicamore-leaf." Upon questioning, the
actor complains of the weakness of his back, and to the
suggestion that he wear a girdle, he replies, "How can a
single Girdle do me good, when a Brace was my Destruction?" The remainder of the conversation is unquotable.[1]

1. Thomas Brown, *Works* (London, 1720), II, 224–225.

VII

On the day of the verdict Luttrell reported that Mrs. Mountfort had brought her appeal. This same information reaching the ears of Mohun, he submitted a petition to the lords, in which he stated that, although he had been acquitted of the charge of murder, "yet one Susannah Percevall, pretending to be Mountford's widow," has procured a writ of appeal against him and "threatens to prosecute it in the Court of King's Bench" at a time, so he apprehends, when the House of Lords is not sitting. He therefore prays their directions. The petition was read on Friday, February 24, and it was then ordered to be considered on the following Monday, at which time the judges were directed to attend. The lords again postponed action until Friday, March 3. On that day, however, after debate, the petition was ordered dismissed because no appeal had actually been brought.[1]

By March the company had sufficiently recovered from the shock of the losses of the end of the previous year to be ready once more to present new plays. In November Thomas Shadwell, one of their most active dramatists, had died; and fifteen days after Mountfort breathed his last, Anthony Leigh was buried in the church of St. Bride's. It was said that the latter's death was caused by a fever brought on by the stabbing of his friend.[2] These blows were severe for the company, and *The Gentleman's Journal*

1. Luttrell, III, 30, 46, 48; *Manuscripts of the House of Lords, 1692–1693*, p. 298; *Journals of the House of Lords*, XV, 247, 251, 272–273.

2. Cibber, I, 154; the "Account" states that Mountfort's death "had so great an Affect on his Dear Companion, Mr. LEE the Comedian, that he did not survive him above the space of a Week." Luttrell gives the date of his death as Wednesday, December 21, but a letter to Anthony Wood, dated December 24, states that Leigh "died on Thursday last (22 Dec.)" (*Life and Times*, III, 412).

of December, 1692 — issued certainly not before January, 1693 [1] — announced: "We are like to be without new Plays this month and the next; the Death of Mr. *Mountfort*, and that of Mr. *Leigh* soon after him, being partly the cause of this delay." Early March, it is probable, was the time when *The Maid's Last Prayer* was presented with Mrs. Mountfort acting Lady Susan Malepert; Mrs. Bracegirdle, the less important Lady Trickitt; and Powell, Granger, the young man about town whom Lady Susan would like to win, — a part of the type that had been frequently taken by Mountfort. Southerne's comedy was followed shortly afterwards by the sweeping triumph of *The Old Batchelour*, in which Mrs. Mountfort also appeared in the longest female rôle, that of the affected Belinda, and Mrs. Bracegirdle was her friend Araminta. Powell essayed Bellmour, who loves Belinda, — a part which Congreve, I think, wrote with Mountfort in mind.[2]

In the next month, the child unborn at the time of its father's death, but mentioned in his will, was baptized at St. Clement Danes on April 27 as "Mary Mumford of William and Susannah uxor." [3] The mother did not re-

1. The November issue, which contains a brief obituary notice of Mountfort, was advertised in *The London Gazette* of December 22–26. The December issue would obviously not be ready before January.

2. The dates of the first performances of *The Maid's Last Prayer* and *The Old Batchelour* are usually placed in January, 1693 — probably because of references in *The Gentleman's Journal*. The January issue mentions the facts that *The Maid's Last Prayer* "was acted the 3d time this evening, and is to be acted again tomorrow," and that Congreve's comedy "will be acted in a little time"; but it should be noted that the first words of the January issue are "We are now in *March*." The February number, published either in late March or early April, refers to the extraordinary success of *The Old Batchelour*.

3. The register of St. Clement Danes also records the baptism on March 22, 1691/2, of "Elizabeth Mumford of William Mumford gent and Susanna uxor," and, on March 30, the burial of "Elizabeth Mumford a chil."

main off the stage for long; before summer she had played Annabella, another "breeches part," in George Powell's *A Very Good Wife* and Catchat, the old maid, in Thomas Wright's *The Female Virtuosos*.[1]

In the autumn Mrs. Mountfort was again in trouble, for on September 10 her father Thomas Percival, who for several years had not appeared upon the stage, was arrested for clipping and sent to Newgate. At the sessions at the Old Bailey held in October, he was sentenced to death. On the very day when Luttrell records this fact, the seventeenth, he also notes that "Mrs. Mountfort hath petitioned the queen for her fathers pardon, which [is] beleived may be granted if she withdraw her appeal against lord Mohun." The plea had its effect: on October 24 we learn that "Percivall and Dear, two clippers, were repreived."[2] One wonders whether Mrs. Mountfort would need to withdraw an appeal against Mohun — if she had made one — in order to gain this kindness from royalty. It seems more likely that Queen Mary, who had felt melancholy and discouraged at Mohun's acquittal, was moved by pity to grant a favor to the widow of her favorite actor.

Shortly after gaining mercy for her father, she again appeared in a play by Congreve as the coquette and pretender to poetry, Lady Froth in *The Double-Dealer*. The last new part she assumed while she bore the name of

1. *A Very Good Wife*, which is mentioned as having been acted five times in the April, 1693, issue of *The Gentleman's Journal* (published probably not before the latter part of May), is advertised for sale in *The London Gazette* of June 15–19, 1693. *The Female Virtuosos* is mentioned as having been performed, in the May issue of *The Gentleman's Journal* (probably published in June) and advertised to be published "tomorrow" in *The London Gazette* of June 22–26, 1693.

2. Luttrell, III, 183, 205, 206, 207, 212.

Mrs. Mountfort was Dalinda in Dryden's final composition
for the theatre, *Love Triumphant*. On January 31, 1694,
the register of St. Clement Danes records the marriage
of "John Verbuggin B. and Susanna Mumford W." The
first reference to her as "Mrs. *Verbruggen*" is to be found
in the quarto of Southerne's *The Fatal Marriage*, a play in
which she spoke the epilogue when it was first performed
in February or March. With Mrs. Mountfort becoming
Mrs. Verbruggen, she passes from our narrative.

It is also not necessary to say much about the future
successes of Mrs. Bracegirdle. As we have seen, only a few
months after the death of Mountfort, she acted in *The Old
Batchelour* and thus began her association with the plays
of that author with whom her name is forever linked. And
in one of the greatest rôles an English comic dramatist ever
wrote for an actress, Millamant, she faced in the passages
of verbal fencing a Mirabell acted by Susannah Mountfort's second husband, Verbruggen.

Lord Mohun's later career was marked by much violence. Before he reached his majority, he had given a cut
on the head to Francis Scobell, who had prevented him
from killing a coachman; he had cudgeled a news-writer
Dyer; he had fought a duel with Captain Bingham; and he
had stabbed Captain William Hill, who died of the wounds.
Although he was indicted for murder and imprisoned because of this act, he was pardoned by the king. In politics
he was a staunch Whig, and by the time he was thirty he
had become a member of the Kit-Cat Club. On November 15, 1712, he and James, the fourth Duke of Hamilton,
who had been involved in lawsuits with each other for ten
years, met in a duel and were both killed.[1]

1. Forsythe, *passim*.

Captain Richard Hill, after giving Mountfort his death-blow, ran up Surrey Street and made good his escape. Rumors were heard at various times that he had been apprehended. On January 19, 1693, word had reached London that he had been taken in the Isle of Wight. On February 7 it was reported that he was a prisoner in Scotland;[1] and on February 6, 1694, a news-letter contained the statement that "Captain Hill, who killed Mr. Mountford, has come from St. Germains and surrendered himself."[2]

Where he was in the years immediately following the actor's death is not known. On December 29, 1692, his company had a new captain in John Simmonds.[3] After the Mountfort affair had blown over, he was recommended by his former commander to Colonel John Gibson, whom he accompanied to Newfoundland as a volunteer in 1697, "in hopes of meeting his Majesty's mercy." Gibson was to report that at this time Hill had never missed an occasion "to signalise his valour, nor did he slip any opportunity to show his zeal for the service."

Early in her reign, Hill presented a petition to Queen Anne, setting forth that he had been "unhappily drawn into a quarrel with Mr. Mountfort wherein he had the misfortune to give him a mortal wound, for which unadvised act [he] has humbled himself before God these eleven years past," and begging her, "in compassion to his youth, to extend [her] Royal mercy to [him] for a crime to which he was betrayed by the heat and folly of youth, that he may thereby be enabled to serve [her] Majestie and his country,

1. Luttrell, III, 15, 31.
2. *Calendar of State Papers, Domestic Series, 1695, and Addenda, 1689–1695*, p. 238.   3. Dalton, III, 270.

as his earnest desire is, to the last drop of his blood." This plea was accompanied by certifications signed by both Erle and Gibson that while under their commands Hill had always acted as a man of honor.[1] A more important military leader than either of these officers was, however, willing to exert himself in the fugitive captain's behalf. Among the manuscripts of the Duke of Portland is another petition to Anne in which it is stated that

in obedience to the Duke of Marlborough's commands, [Hill] served this campaign in Germany as a volunteer, and being wounded in the last glorious victory [Blenheim], had leave to return to throw himself at her Majesty's feet to pray for pardon — in compassion to his youth, in pity to his wife and five small children, and in regard to his services — for a crime committed at sixteen years of age and eleven years since.

On September 3, 1704, Marlborough sent a letter to Harley, forwarding a memorial signed by six of his general officers on behalf of Hill, "representing his good behaviour in the two late actions and recommending him as a fit object of her Majesty's mercy." [2] It seems likely that he was eventually pardoned and that he was the Captain Richard Hill whom the Duke of Ormonde recommended for a commission in the "New Levies" in 1706.[3]

1. Dalton, IV, 297–298.
2. *Manuscripts of the Duke of Portland* (Historical Manuscripts Commission), VIII, 321–322. It is possible that he is the same Hill who wrote Harley on May 13, 1705, about the queen's bounty money and also sent a letter to be forwarded to Marlborough. In the latter he indicates his pitiable plight: "he is so reduced in circumstances that he blushes to own that he was forced to dispose of something off his back to carry him down to the country to try if he could raise as much money as would equip him for his Grace's generosity. But, being forced to go threescore miles afoot, it pleased God to throw him into a violent ague and fever, and till now has not been able to put pen to paper, but will make hard shift to be soon after his Grace" (*idem*, 182).
3. Dalton, IV, 298.

In the previous year a tragedy called *Zelmane: Or, The Corinthian Queen* was published. It had been presented at the theatre in Lincoln's Inn Fields with Verbruggen, Booth, Mrs. Barry, and Mrs. Bracegirdle in the principal parts, and "the Town [had] been favourable in its Character." No author's name appeared upon the title-page, but the writer of the unsigned dedication said that the "following Poem was a piece left unfinished by Mr. M——t, who in his Life was generally belov'd, and encourag'd in what he did by all," and that he hoped "the memory of the Author [might] excuse the defects of [his] Addition." "M——t" has been assumed to mean "Mountfort," [1] mistakenly I believe. If this were actually the re-working of an unfinished tragedy by a writer who had also been a player and two of whose comedies were not yet dead as acting drama, it seems strange that there is no mention of that fact in the prologue or epilogue, especially since the two leading female parts were taken by women who had appeared with Mountfort on many occasions. It also seems unreasonable to suppose that the writer of the dedicatory epistle would be timid about spelling out the name of the author, had he been Mountfort. In fact, the words — "in his Life . . . generally belov'd, and encourag'd in what he did by all" — do not, in my opinion, refer to a

---

1. No author is indicated in "List of all the English Dramatic Poets" printed with Thomas Whincop's *Scanderbeg* (1747), [Chetwood's] *The British Theatre* (1752), and Dodsley's *Theatrical Records* (1756). David E. Baker, in *The Companion to the Play-House* (1764), writes, "*Coxeter* in his *MS*. tells us it was left unfinish'd by Mr. M——t (probably Mr. *Mountfort*) but does not inform us by whom it was finished." Coxeter's suggestion that "Mr. M——t" is "probably Mr. *Mountfort*" is apparently the only reason for attributing the play to Mountfort, and a very flimsy reason it is. Despite the fact that the editions of the *Biographia Dramatica* in 1782 and in 1812 repeat the statement of Coxeter, they list *Zelmane* without any qualifications among the plays of Mountfort.

person who passed his writing career in the hurly-burly of the theatre, but rather to one who composed his lines for a group of kindly disposed, but not too severely critical, friends. That *Zelmane* was not generally considered to be the work of Mountfort is also clear from the fact that it was not printed in 1720 in the collected edition of his plays, which contained four pieces by him and the two historical tragedies by Bancroft.

The materials contained in the brief account of the author prefixed to the first of these two volumes have been used elsewhere in this study. The final statement alone remains for consideration: the reference to the fact that Mountfort "left two Daughters; one whereof is an excellent Actress, but she has lately quitted the Stage." The daughters were Susanna, the record of whose baptism I have been unable to find,[1] and the posthumous Mary. Of the latter nothing is known. The former made a name for herself in the theatre of the early part of the eighteenth century. Beginning as a member of the company at Lincoln's Inn Fields, she later acted at Drury Lane and was the first to appear as Rose in *The Recruiting Officer*. Among the rôles which she played of those originally taken

1. I have searched in vain the baptismal records of St. Martin's in the Fields, St. Giles in the Fields, St. Bride's, and St. Clement Danes. For completeness a bit of theatrical gossip related by *The Stage Veteran* ought to be noted: "It was remembered by old actors as a tradition current sixty years ago, that the motive for the murder of Mountfort was not jealousy of Mrs. Bracegirdle's attachment to him, but revenge for his having gained and betrayed the affections of a lady of exceedingly high rank in this county, and that one of the children whom Mrs. Mountfort brought up as her own, was in fact the fruits of the amour in question. That child was living in 1730" (Percy Fitzgerald, *A New History of the English Stage*, I, 195–196n.). For Susanna Mountfort's amour with Booth, see pp. 28–33 of Theophilus Cibber, *The Life and Character of . . . Barton Booth*, contained in Part I of *The Lives and Characters of the most Eminent Actors and Actresses of Great Britain and Ireland* (London, 1753).

by her mother were Belinda in *The Old Batchelour*, Hypo-
lita in *She wou'd, and she wou'd not*, and Lady Brumpton
in *The Funeral*. There is no evidence that she ever had a
part in the revivals of either of her father's comedies. She
was to be the mistress of the tragedian Barton Booth and
finally to leave the stage when she became mentally in-
capacitated.

The record of the life and death of William Mountfort
now comes to an end. Beginning as a boy before the union
of the companies, he advanced from minor rôles to leading
parts, his specialties in tragedy being unfortunate lovers
and in comedy witty young men about town. As a fop he
was without rival, and when occasion offered he could act
the villain also. His impersonations were especially pleasing to the feminine part of the audience, including Queen
Mary, whose favorite actor he was. Not encouraged by
Betterton in the early part of his career, he had attained,
at the end of his brief life, a position among the actors
second only to that occupied by the older man. His successor in portraying fops was Cibber, and in presenting
lovers and rakes he was followed by Powell and Wilks.
The latter — it was reported [1] — resolved, upon hearing
of Mountfort's death, to leave Ireland for England at the
first opportunity.

During his career as an actor, he was able to write three
original plays, to convert a tragedy into a farce, and to
assist his friends now and then by supplying scenes for
their works. After an experiment in tragedy, *The Injur'd
Lovers*, he found that his vein lay in plays of a lighter character where witty dialogue and boisterous fun were of

1. Cibber, I, 237.

paramount importance. In *The Successful Strangers* and *Greenwich Park* he was at his best in the scenes which he wrote for himself, his wife, and the three comedians, Leigh, Nokes, and Underhill, although in Dorinda he drew for Mrs. Barry one of his finest portraits. His two comedies share with the dramatic works of Cibber the distinction of being probably the best plays written by actors during the last quarter of the seventeenth century. In addition to contriving good characterizing dialogue, Mountfort could pen gracefully turned lyrics, and he was ready, when occasion demanded, with a prologue or epilogue.

When all is said and done, his position in the history of the English drama lies primarily in his ability as an actor. Thanks to Colley Cibber, some idea of what that ability was has been passed on to readers nearly two hundred and fifty years after his last appearance at Drury Lane. And so, after bringing to a conclusion my extended footnote on the career of William Mountfort, I am ready once more to take my copy of the *Apology* from the shelf and turn to the fifth chapter.

APPENDIXES

APPENDIXES

APPENDIX A

MOUNTFORT'S USE OF MARLOWE'S *DOCTOR FAUSTUS*

Marlowe's play of *Doctor Faustus* was first entered in the Stationers' Register on January 7, 1601, by Thomas Bushell. On September 13, 1610, it was assigned by him to John Wright. On June 27, 1646, by order of a "Court of Assistants" held on the previous April 6, it was made over to his brother Edward Wright; and on April 4, 1655, the latter assigned it to William Gilbertson.

The earliest extant edition printed for Bushell is dated 1604. With a few variants, this text was reproduced in 1609 for John Wright and again in 1611. In 1616 Wright brought out a considerably expanded text without any indication upon the title-page that new material had been added. This deficiency was remedied in 1619 when the words "With new Additions" first appeared. With a few variants the edition was again issued in 1620, 1624, and 1631. Then, after a lapse of thirty-two years, Gilbertson in 1663 brought out "The Tragicall History of the Life and Death of Doctor Faustus. Printed with New Additions as it is now Acted. With several New Scenes, together with the Actors Names. Written by Ch. Mar." One might naturally assume that this edition, which was the last to appear in the seventeenth century, was used by Mountfort as a basis for his farce.

It is now necessary to examine a few passages as they appear in the farce (published in 1697) and in the editions of 1663 and 1631:

O *Faustus!* lay that damn'd Book aside;
And gaze not on it, lest it tempt thy heart to blasphemy.

(1697 ed., p. 1)

O *Faustus* lay that damned book aside,
And gaze not on it, least it tempt thy heart to blasphemy,

(1663 ed., sig. A3)

O *Faustus*, lay that damned booke aside,
And gaze not on it, lest it tempt thy soule,
And heape Gods heauy wrath vpon thy head.
Read, read the Scriptures: that is blasphemy.

(1631 ed., sigs. A3, A3ᵛ)

That I shall wait on *Faustus* whil'st he Lives,
So thou wilt buy my Service with thy Blood.

(1697 ed., p. 4)

That I shall wait on *Faustus* whilst he lives,
So thou will buy his service with thy blood

(1663 ed., sig. B3ᵛ)

That I shall wait on *Faustus* whilst he liues,
So he will buy my seruice with his soule.

(1631 ed., sig. B3ᵛ)

Ay, but thou must bequeath it solemnly,
And write a Deed of Gift with it;   (1697 ed., p. 4)

But now thou must bequeath it solemnly,
And write a deed of Gift with it,   (1663 ed., sig. B3ᵛ)

But now thou must bequeath it solemnly,
And write a Deed of Gift with thine owne blood:

(1631 ed., sig. B3ᵛ)

Meph. . . . this is: Thou art Lost; think thou of Hell.
Faust.   Think, *Faustus*, upon him that made the World.

(1697 ed., p. 6)

Meph. . . . This is: thou art lost, think thou of Hell.
Faust.   Think *Faustus* upon him that made the world.

(1663 ed., sig. C2ᵛ)

Meph. . . . This is: thou art damn'd, thinke thou of Hell.
Faust.   Thinke *Faustus* vpon God that made the world.

(1631 ed., sig. C2ᵛ)

Luc. Thou call'st on Heav'n contrary to thy Promise.
Beel. Thou should'st not think on Heav'n.

(1697 ed., p. 10)

Luci. Thou cal'st on heaven contrary to thy promise.
Belz. Thou shouldst not think on heaven.

(1663 ed., sig. C3)

Luci. Thou calst on Christ contrary to thy promise.
Belz. Thou shouldst not thinke on God.

(1631 ed., sig. C3)

I'll ne'er trust Smooth-face and Small-band more:

(1697 ed., p. 21)

Ile nere trust soomth [*sic*] faces, and small bands more:

(1663 ed., sig. E3ᵛ)

I'le nere trust smooth faces, and small ruffes more.

(1631 ed., sig. E4ᵛ)

Thus from the infernal *Dis* do we ascend, bringing
with us the Deed; the Time is come which makes
it forfeit.   (1697 ed., p. 24)

Thus from infernal *Dis* do we ascend,
Bringing with us the Deed
The time is come; which makes it forfeit

(1663 ed., sig. G3ᵛ)

Thus from infernall *Dis* doe we ascend,
To view the subiects of our monarchie,
Those soules which sinne seales the black sonnes of hell,
Mongst which as chiefe, *Faustus* we come to thee,
Bringing with vs lasting damnation,
To wait vpon thy soule; the time is come
Which makes it forfeit.   (1631 ed., sig. G4ᵛ)

   In the passages just cited Mountfort was evidently following the text of the edition of 1663. Other lines, however, seem
to indicate that he also had before him one of the reprints of
the 1616 edition, possibly that of 1631.

   Why shouldst thou not? Is not thy Soul thy own?

(1697 ed., p. 5)

Why shouldst thou not? is not thy soule thine owne?
(1631 ed., sig. B4)

Why shouldst thou not? is it not thine own?
(1663 ed., sig. B4)

What is't I would not do to obtain his Soul?
(1697 ed., p. 5)

What will not I doe to obtaine his soule?
(1631 ed., sig. B4)

What will I not do to obtain this man?
(1663 ed., sig. B4)

. . . a Plague take him,   (1697 ed., p. 17)

. . . a plague take him,   (1631 ed., sig. F4)

. . . a pox take him,   (1663 ed., sig. F3)

But I have it again now I am awake.
(1697 ed., p. 19)

But I haue it againe now I am awake? looke you here sir.
(1631 ed., sig. G2ᵛ)

But I have it again now? look you here sir.
(1663 ed., sig. G1ᵛ)

O wondrous Sight!   (1697 ed., p. 20)

O wondrous sight!   (1631 ed., sig. E4)

O wonderful sight!   (1663 ed., sig. E3)

A plausible generalization from these quotations would be that Mountfort used as the principal source for his farce the edition of 1663, but that in some instances he chose the wording of an earlier text. Such a procedure seems unlikely. The Restoration writer's merciless slashing of *Dr. Faustus* until it becomes a mere skeleton does not lead me to believe that he would bother to balance the possibilities as to which of two readings for a given line is the better.

I am ready to venture the suggestion that sometime between 1631 and 1663, an edition of the Elizabethan play was printed which represents an intermediate stage between the editions of these two years, and that this edition was used by Mountfort. It has been noted that the play was assigned to Edward Wright in 1646. No edition with his name is extant. It has also been noted that the play became the property of Gilbertson in 1655. The first extant printing made for him was in 1663. May not Edward Wright have issued the play sometime between 1646 and 1655 or may not Gilbertson have brought out an edition before the end of the eight years which elapsed between 1655 and 1663? Of course, the suggestion that there was a "lost edition" is merely conjecture, but it seems a more likely explanation of the wording of the 1697 text than that the author of the farce used two editions.

Mountfort's use of the earlier play is indicated briefly in what follows. Act I begins with Faustus in his study. Marlowe's opening soliloquy of some sixty lines is cut to eight. Then the Good Angel and the Bad Angel enter with their pleas, which closely follow the original. After again soliloquizing briefly, Faustus begins to conjure with lines adapted from Marlowe's third scene. What follows is Mountfort's work. Mephostopholis (Mephostophilis in 1631 and 1663 editions) speaks from under the ground. There is a flash of light, and Scaramouche enters frightened. After being terrified by a devil, he is taken into the doctor's service and set to work cleaning the study. With the entrance of Mephostopholis, Marlowe's play is again used. Materials from the third and the fifth scenes are telescoped in such a way that one sequence contains Mephostopholis' promise to do what Faustus commands, Faustus' readiness to resign his soul to Lucifer in exchange for twenty-four years of living in all voluptuousness, the congealing of his blood as he attempts to write, the pleas of the two Angels, the bringing of the chafer of fire, Faustus' seeing "Homo, fuge" on his arm, the devils' presenting crowns to the doctor, the delivering of the deed of gift, and Faustus' demand for a wife. He would behold "the Famous *Hellen*, who was the Occasion of great *Troys* Destruction." Mephostopholis waves his wand, and she enters. Marlowe's poetry is reduced to these pedestrian lines:

> *Faust.* O *Mephostopholis!* what would I give to gain a Kiss from off those lovely Lips.
> *Meph.* *Faustus*, thou may'st. [*He kisses her.*
> *Faust.* My Soul is fled; come *Hellen*, come, give me my Soul again; she's gon. [*He goes to kiss her again, and she sinks.*

Mephostopholis describes hell: "'tis Glorious as the upper World; but that we have Night and Day, as you have here: Above, there's no Night." Faustus, as in Marlowe, thinks "Hell's a meer Fable," and asks questions concerning who made the world. Here material is taken from both the fifth and sixth scenes of the earlier treatment. Faustus is ready to repent; he goes to his books and finds "This Bible's fast, but here's another." Then comes the direction: "*They both fly out of's Hand, and a flaming Thing appears written*, &c." The scene is brought to a close with the coming of the Good and the Bad Angels as in Marlowe. The remainder of the act is Mountfort's.

Act II also begins with Faustus in his study, and the text again is based on Marlowe's sixth scene. The Good and the Bad Angels descend and make their persuading and dissuading speeches, but Faustus' heart is hardened, and he cannot repent. Then Lucifer, Beelzebub, and Mephostopholis rise; because of their protest, Faustus vows never to look to heaven. The Seven Deadly Sins appear and give their characters, but their speeches are considerably changed from those in Marlowe. Lucifer tells Faustus that in hell are all manner of delights, and that he will show him the mighty pleasures in the world below. The concluding scenes in the act are by Mountfort.

Act III begins in a wood. Twelve years have passed, during which time Faustus has seen the utmost limits of the spacious world. The Good and the Bad Angels are again at hand with their customary speeches. With the entrance of the Horse-

courser Marlowe's text is used: he complains that his horse
has been turned to straw, he pulls off Faustus' leg and is terrified, he and the Carter tell of their experiences with the magician
and depart without paying for their ale. They are fluently
cursed by the Hostess — an addition by Mountfort. Eight
years elapse. The Old Man begs Faustus to give up his evil
ways. Mephostopholis is soon at hand to call the doctor traitor
and to threaten to tear him to pieces. This scene follows Marlowe fairly closely, but with many omissions. The Horse-
courser and the Carter come to drink a health to Faustus'
wooden leg. As in Marlowe, Faustus assures them he has his
leg again, waves his wand, and silences all who make demands
of him. He is next at the palace of the Emperor, who wishes to
behold Alexander fighting with Darius. Benoolio [Benuolio in
Marlowe] has his doubts, acquires his horns, and is ordered by
the magician to speak well of scholars in the future. In recom-
pense for gratifying his wish, the Emperor will let Faustus command the state of Germany. This passage follows the earlier
version with omissions and some changes of phraseology. The
next scene is the garden where, as in Marlowe, Benoolio cuts
Faustus' false head off. Faustus calls his devils and orders them
to drag Benoolio and his comrades through the mud and dirt.
Mountfort's scene in the hall where Scaramouche acts as steward follows. Marlowe's text of the next to the last scene is then
used. Lucifer, Beelzebub, and Mephostopholis bring the deed,
which is now forfeit. The Old Man begs Faustus to call on
heaven, but the doctor assures him that it is too late and
turns upon Mephostopholis, who rejoices. The Good and the
Bad Angels show him heaven and hell with due admonitions.
An abbreviated version of the great soliloquy is given, after
which Faustus sinks with the devils. The Old Man and the
Scholar enter (instead of Marlowe's two scholars) and discover
Faustus' limbs; whereupon the Old Man pronounces Mountfort's moralistic epilogue:

    May this a fair Example be to all,
    To avoid such Ways which brought poor *Faustus*'s Fall.
    And whatsoever Pleasure does invite,
    Sell not your Souls to purchase vain Delight.

The scene changes to hell, where the limbs come together, and
the farce is concluded with a dance and song.

APPENDIX B

THEATRICAL HISTORY OF MOUNTFORT'S PLAYS

The materials for the following account of the eighteenth century performances of Mountfort's plays are found in Genest's
Some Account of the English Stage and in the Latreille Manuscript (British Museum Additional MSS. 32249–32252).

I

DOCTOR FAUSTUS

    The farce was revived at the theatre in Lincoln's Inn Fields
"with Songs and Dances between the Acts" in 1697, but no
cast has been preserved. The names of the actors who appeared
in the performances at the Little Theatre in the Haymarket
more than twenty-five years later are also not known. On November 26, 1723, there was presented at Drury Lane, as an
afterpiece to *Rule A Wife and Have a Wife*, a pantomime by
the dancing-master John Thurmond entitled *Harlequin Doctor
Faustus: With the Masque of the Deities*. Emboldened by the
success, the company at the Haymarket put on as a rival attraction, on January 31, 1724, the "original play of the Life
and Death of Dr. Faustus — With the humours of Harlequin
and Scaramouch — written by Mr. Mountfort, With sinkings,
flyings, dances, and other decorations proper to the same."
With this was given Henry Carey's two-act farce, *The Con-*

trivances; or More Ways than One. These two farces were repeated on February 1 and February 4. On February 18, at Williams' benefit, Mountfort's play served as an afterpiece to Mrs. Centlivre's *Marplot.*

W. R. Chetwood, *A General History of the Stage* (London, 1749), p. 139, tells of an accident that "fell out in Dr. *Faustus,* a Pantomime Entertainment in *Lincoln's-Inn-Fields* Theatre, where a Machine in the Working broke, threw the mock *Pierrot* down headlong with such Force, that the poor Man broke a Plank on the Stage with his Fall, and expired: Another was so sorely maimed, that he did not survive many Days; and a third, one of the softer Sex, broke her Thigh. But to prevent such Accidents for the future, those Persons are represented by inanimate Figures, so that if they break a Neck, a Leg, or an Arm, there needs no Surgeon."

II

THE SUCCESSFUL STRANGERS

During the summer season of 1708 this play was given at Drury Lane on July 20 and 22, as "not acted 15 years," with an entirely different cast from that which appeared at the first performances: Silvio = Mills, Antonio = Booth, Carlos = Husband, Don Lopez = Norris, Don Francisco = Bullock, Don Pedro = Cross, Sancho = Pack, Guzman = Fairbank, Dorothea = Mrs. Porter, Feliciana = Mrs. Bradshaw, Biancha = Miss Norris, Farmosa = Mrs. Powell.

It was revived for the benefit of Mrs. Moor, "at the desire of several persons of quality" on January 31, 1710. Booth, Norris, and Pack retained the parts they had played in 1708, and Mrs. Knight, who had acted Dorothea when the comedy was first given in 1690, once more assumed that rôle. The remainder of the cast follows: Don Francisco = Spiller, Don Pedro = Layfield, Silvio = Powell, Carlos = Elrington, Guzman = Miller,

Feliciana = Mrs. Moor, Biancha = Mrs. Spiller, Niece = Mrs. Cox. The play was also presented during the summer season of 1711 on June 29, with Bullock Junior playing Guzman.

The last performances of this comedy were possibly those at the theatre in Lincoln's Inn Fields on June 25 and 28, 1728. The receipts at the first were £10 11s., and at the second, £11 5s. The cast was: Silvio = Milward, Antonio = Berriman, Don Francisco = Bullock, Don Carlos = Ogden, Don Lopez = Smith, Don Pedro = Pitt, Don Octavio = Houghton, Surgeon = H. Bullock, Guzman = Gifford, Sancho = Clark, Dorothea = Mrs. Berriman, Feliciana = Miss Tynte, Biancha = Miss Palin, Farmosa = Mrs. Martin, Niece = Miss Anderson. These presentations were accompanied by "several entertainments of singing and dancing, — particularly 'In the merry month of May' by Miss Warren, end of Act 2nd; — a Scottish dance by Smith and Mrs. Ogden, end of Act 3. Singing by Salway in Act 4. And dancing by Miss Labour at the end of the Play."

III

GREENWICH PARK

Mountfort's last play held the stage for fifty years. On April 22, 1704, after not being acted for four years, it was presented at Drury Lane "at the desire of several persons of quality." Performances at that theatre followed on April 26, 1704, and on March 1 and December 21, 1705. Then on April 17, 1708, it was given by Her Majesties United Company of Comedians. Two of those who had played in the original cast, Bowen and Mrs. Knight, were continued in their old rôles of Sir William Thoughtless and Mrs. Raison. The others were: Lord Worthy = Mills, Sir Thomas Reveller = Pinkethman, Young Reveller = Cibber, Raison = Johnson, Sassafras = Bullock, Bounce = Fairbank, Beau = Pack, Florella = Mrs. Oldfield, Violante = Mrs. Moor, Dorinda = Mrs. Rogers, Aunt =

Mrs. Powell. This cast appeared also on April 20, October 18, and December 29, 1708.

The comedy in a "carefully revised" version was advertised to be given on June 21, 1715, but on account of the hot weather the performance was postponed until June 24. It was repeated on July 1. Bickerstaffe had now succeeded to the part of Lord Worthy, Miller to Sir Thomas Reveller, Mills to Young Reveller, Shepherd to Sassafras, Mrs. Porter to Florella, Mrs. Horton to Dorinda, Mrs. Cox to Violante, Mrs. Baker to the Aunt, and Mrs. Saunders to Mrs. Raison. To add to the interest there was singing in Italian by young Bowman, the Country Dialogue of Roger and Dolly by Renton and Mrs. Willis, and dancing by Miss Younger. When, on July 15, it was again given "at the desire of several persons of quality," Miss Younger played Florella.

It was also acted on January 4, February 8, May 2, and November 14, 1716. At the latter presentation, Pinkethman assumed once more his old rôle of Sir Thomas Reveller. The performance on February 11, 1717, was by His Royal Highness's comm nd, and that on May 27, 1717 — advertised as *The Humorous old Rake or Greenwich Park* — was for the benefit of Tom D'Urfey, on which occasion the aging playwright and song-writer spoke "a new oration on several famous heads for the entertainment of the Court and the Audience his friends."

In 1718 it could be seen on February 6, May 28, and November 28. At the second of these performances, which was a benefit for Weller, Higginson, and Mrs. Bowman, Dorinda was taken by Mrs. Moor and Violante by Miss Willis; at the third, Lord Worthy was played by Thurmond and Dorinda once more by Mrs. Horton. On November 23, 1719, Miss Teno acted Violante.

At the Haymarket it was given on December 26, 1723, as "not acted 6 years," and repeated on December 27 and 30.

Drury Lane, on October 10, 1730, revived *Greenwich Park; or The Merry Citizens* with an excellent cast: Sir Thomas

Reveller = Harper, Young Reveller = Cibber, Raison = Johnson, Sassafras = Shepherd, Lord Worthy = Bridgewater, Dorinda = Mrs. Horton, Florella = Mrs. Booth, Violante = Mrs. Butler, Lady Hazard = Mrs. Grace, Mrs. Raison = Mrs. Mills, Aunt = Mrs. Wetherilt. The same players repeated their performance with Charles Coffey's ballad opera, *The Beggar's Wedding*, on October 13, and with Henry Carey's farce, *The Contrivances*, on October 15.

On December 3, 1730, it was presented for the benefit of Henry Carey, "with some additional songs, proper to the characters, which will be printed and given gratis to all persons at their entrance. And several other entertainments of singing — particularly a Dialogue of Mr. Henry Purcell's by Mr. Carey and Miss Raftor and a Cantata of Mr. Carey's by Miss Raftor — with entertainments of Dancing." In order to arouse interest in the benefit performance, *The Daily Post* printed this statement: "Our Friend Henry Carey having this night a benefit at Drury Lane Play House the powers of music, painting, and poetry assemble in his behalf, he being an admirer of the Three sister Arts. The body of Musicians meet in the Haymarket from whence they march in great order preceded by a magnificent moving organ in form of a Pageant, accompanied by all kinds of musical instruments ever in use from Tubal Cain to this day. A great multitude of Booksellers, Authors and Printers form themselves into a body at Temple Bar from whence they march with great decency to Covent Garden preceded by a little Army of Printer's devils with their proper implements. Here the two bodies of Music and Painting are joined by the Brothers of the Pencil where, taking a glass of refreshment at the Bedford Arms, they make a solemn procession to the Theatre amidst an innumerable crowd of spectators." It was also given on December 28, 1730, and on April 23, 1731, at the benefit of Watson and Mrs. Butler. On November 12, 1731, it was acted "By their Majesties Command" and followed by

Lacy Ryan's ballad opera, *The Amours of Billingsgate*. When it was presented with Charles Coffey's ballad opera, *The Devil to Pay*, on December 17, 1731, and October 21, 1732, Mrs. Charke played Mrs. Raison.

The cast on November 10, 1735, was — with the exception of Harper, Johnson, Shepherd, and Mrs. Butler — made up of performers who were new to their parts: Worthy = Salway, Young Reveller = W. Mills, Florella = Mrs. Thurmond, Dorinda = Mrs. Pritchard, Lady Hazard = Mrs. Canbrell, Mrs. Raison = Mrs. Cross. On November 11, with *Harlequin Restored*, it was given "for the entertainment of His Highness the Duke of Modena." It was acted also on December 27, 1735, and February 27, 1736. (Genest says that Cibber Junior played Young Reveller at the latter performance.) The same cast appeared on October 29, 1736, with the exception of Este as Lord Worthy and Mrs. Grace as Lady Hazard. This appears to have been the last performance at Drury Lane.

It was acted at Covent Garden on January 29, 1741, for the first time, and repeated on January 31, February 2, February 3, February 6 "By Command of the Prince and Princess of Wales," and April 15. The cast was excellent: Sir Thomas Reveller = Hippisley, Lord Worthy = Bridgewater (Gibson from February 2), Young Reveller = Hale, Raison = Rosco, Sassafras = Mullart, Steward = Arthur, Lady Hazard = Mrs. Cross, Dorinda = Mrs. Mullart, Violante = Mrs. Bellamy, Mrs. Raison = Mrs. Vincent, Aunt = Mrs. James, Florella = Mrs. Woffington.

APPENDIX C

MS. EGERTON 2623, FOLS. 46–50

Fols. 46–50 of MS. Egerton 2623 are described as "The original and unprinted depositions of witnesses in the case of the Murder of Mountford the Actor by Lord Mohun for the love of Mrs.

Bracegirdle the Actress; with a M.S. Elegy upon Mountford."
The elegy is the work of Tom Brown, and with a few verbal
changes appears as "The Ladies Lamentation for their Adonis"
in the collected edition of his works. MS. Egerton 2623, which
contains papers dealing largely with the English drama, was
purchased for the British Museum by Quaritch at the Ellis sale
in 1885. It had formerly belonged to Frederic Ouvry, at one
time president of the Society of Antiquaries, to whose hands it
had very likely passed from John Payne Collier. (For Collier's
use of fols. 15–18 of this manuscript, see W. W. Greg, "A Collier
Mystification" in *The Review of English Studies*, I [1925]
452–454.)

Collier refers to the material contained in fols. 46–49 and
makes a few quotations from it in his unpublished manuscript
history of the London stage from 1660 to 1723, now in the
Theatre Collection of the Harvard College Library. There he
describes the document as "the original depositions of all the
principal witnesses, taken on the very next day [i.e. December
10, 1692] (before the Privy Council & two days prior to the
Coroner's Inquest), some of whom were not called on the trial
of one of the parties." He also states that the manuscript had
once belonged to the Marquis of Halifax and is endorsed "Concerning Lord Mohun" in his handwriting.

Neither the published account of the trial nor the journal of
the House of Lords contains any indication that witnesses of
the killing of Mountfort were summoned before the Privy Council. The Privy Council Register (P.R.O. P.C. 2/75) is also
silent on the subject. It is, however, evident that these depositions — if they are genuine — were taken on the morning following the fatal stabbing and thus "two days prior to the Coroner's Inquest." They represent, it seems to me, a copy of the
information taken before the justices of the County of Middlesex sitting at Hicks Hall, St. John's Street, Clerkenwell. In a
petition directed to the House of Lords on January 11, 1693,

Mohun states that on December 10 he was "carried before the Justices at Hicks' Hall touching the supposed murder of Mr. Wm. Mountford, where three of the Justices took the examinations of 13 witnesses, none of which could charge Petitioner with the murder" (*Manuscripts of the House of Lords, 1692–3*, p. 294). The number of witnesses whose sworn depositions appear in the manuscript is exactly thirteen: Thomas Leak, Dorothy Browne, Anne Jones, Elizabeth Walker, John Warrington, John Davenport, William Merry, John Bancroft, Ann Rudd, Anne Bracegirdle, Gowen Page, Mary Page, and Martha Bracegirdle. Their depositions and the examination of Lord Mohun, who was not under oath, are unsigned in the manuscript and are all written in the same hand. These are followed by an unsworn statement of Ann Nevitt [Knevitt] written in another hand and undated.

These sheets are probably a copy of the information taken before the justices made at the request of the Marquis of Halifax. On January 14, 1693, he reported to the House of Lords from the Committee for Privileges that they do not find any precedent for a peer's trial except in Westminster Hall, and that they are of opinion that the coroner's inquest taken against Mohun should be sent for. It is not unlikely — although we have no evidence of the fact — that at their deliberations the committee wished also to examine the depositions sworn on the day following the stabbing. A copy would therefore be made. After the trial and acquittal of Mohun, the document probably remained among Halifax's papers. After the death of the marquis, his papers were not preserved intact. Some of them were destroyed; some found their way into the possession of the Cavendish family; others are in the Spencer archives; a large part of the official correspondence has totally disappeared. (See the preface to H. C. Foxcroft, *The Life and Letters of Sir George Savile, Bart. First Marquis of Halifax* [London, 1898].) With a collection thus scattered, it was possible for a stray item, such as these depositions, to be separated from the rest of the fold and finally to become the possession of John Payne Collier.

Of course everything that has passed through the hands of Collier is open to suspicion, and there is the possibility that these depositions are forgeries. But it seems unlikely that Collier would manufacture more than a dozen depositions for the purpose of using four of them in a theatrical history. H. Idris Bell, Esq., Keeper of the Manuscripts, British Museum, writes me that he does not think "there can be any reasonable doubt as to the genuineness of Egerton MS. 2623, ff. 46–50." Professor Leslie Hotson, who has kindly examined the manuscript at my request, also feels that it is an authentic seventeenth-century piece of work. I have been able to find nothing in these depositions that is materially inconsistent with the testimony presented in the published account of the trial.

The contents of fols. 46–49 follow. All the entries except the last — the statement of Ann Nevitt — are in the same hand. It is often difficult to determine whether a capital or a small _s_ is intended. Periods under superior letters have been omitted.

The Information of Thomas Leak taken upon Oath the Tenth Day of Decemb Anno Domini 1692

This Informant Saith that He is Servant to Cap^{tn} Richard Hill and waited on him last night, And the Lord Charles Mohun and the Said Cap^{tn} were together then at the Horse Shoe Taverne in Drury Lane and came thence about Ten of Clock, and there was a Coach and Six Souldiers that attended in Drury lane neare the S^d Taverne., And Mrs Bracegirdle a Player in their Maj^{ties} Play House Coming from that end of Drury Lane furthest from the Strand towards the place where the S^d Coach Stood the S^d Lord and the Cap^{tn} mett the S^d player who was on Foot and lead by a Gent^l whose name this Inform^t has Since heard was Page., And after One of the Said Souldiers had taken the S^d Player in his Arme to get Her into the S^d Coach Mr Page Endeavouring to hinder it, the S^d Cap^{tn} Drew his Sword and Struck the S^d Page ouer the Head, And the Player crying out the Rabble gathered about the Coach, And the Cap^{tn} bid the Souldiers let Her goe., And My Lord

told him Mr. Mountford was killed, and this Informant saw Mr. Watkins go into
Howard Street and the said Hickson was standing there with his sword in its scabbard and
this Informant coming near the said Lord he desired this Informant to take notice that he
was not concerned in Mr. Mountford's death, and the said Lord thereupon delivered his
sword to the Constable and rendered himself to the watch and this Informant saith that Mr.
Mountford's House is very near Mrs. Bracegirdle's Lodgings.

The Information of Martha Bracegirdle widow taken
with Bath of Day and year aforesaid.

This Informant saith that she and her Daughter Anne Bracegirdle and her son Hamlet
Bracegirdle having supt last night at Mr. Page's in Covent Garden and coming from
thence about ten o'clock and walking homewards were stopt in Drury Lane by
severall Souldiers who endeavoured to thrust this Informant's Daughter into a Coach
wherein my Lord Mohun then was and this Informant soon after saw Captain Hill strike
William Page and thereupon a Multitude of People flocking about them, the
said Captain ordered the souldiers to desist from prosecuting their ill Enterprise, and
this Informant saith that afterwards the said Captain accompanyed this Informant and
her Company to their Lodgings in Howard Street and as they were going
thither the said Captain told this Informant he would have revenge, and this Informant soon
after they arrived to the said Lodgings she saw my Lord Mohun in that street
there with the said Captain and the said Lord thereupon told this Informant that she needed
not fear for he had not designed her ill but what was Honble and this Informant farther
saith that about 12 o'clock at night which was an hour after the said Lord spoke
with this Informant as aforesaid she observed the said Lord and Captain Hill walking up and
down in the street before the door of her Lodgings and this Informant took notice
that the said Captain's sword was drawne and that the said Lord Mohun's sword was
not drawne.

Ann Noriot lives in the house over against Mrs. Bracegirdle's
Lodgeings, says that when Captain Hill brought Mrs. Bracegirdle home, the
doore was shutt against him, and that he desired of Mrs. Bracegirdle's
Mother that he might see or speake with her daughter to aske
her pardon that was refused and the Captain and my Lord Mohun
walkt upon the flaggs before her Lodgeings and Severall times,
as they walkt by knocke at the doore and desir'd they might
either see or speake with Mrs. Bracegirdle to aske her pardon and
they would be gone and if it would not be granted they would

and the Cap^{tn} went with Her to Howard Street where (this Inform^t has been Inform'd) the S^d Player Lodged., and ye S^d Cap^{tn} put Her into her Lodgings and Mr Page went in after Her., And My L^d and ye Cap^{tn} Stayd in the Street there about an hour and halfe., And Sent this Inform^t to the white Horse Taverne where they had been before., They went to ye Horse Shoe Taverne for a Bottle of Canary and the Drawer brought it, and My L^d and ye Cap^{tn} Dranck of it in the Street, And Soon after Mr William Mountford came with his Sword Ouer his Arm and went to My L^d and S^d he was Sorry he would Justify Mr Hill's rudeness, And then the Cap^{tn} cam[e] to Him and S^d he would Justify Himselfe and went towards the Middle of the Street and Mr Mountford followed Him and Drew, the Cap^{tn} having his Sword in his Hand the Sccabbard being lost in the affray with Mr Page and they made passes at each other And Mr Mountford Said Soon after he has kill'd mee, and the Cap^{tn} fled And this Inform^t went after him and lost Him about Covent Garden and then went to the Cap$^{tn's}$ Lodgings in Buckingham Court but the Cap^{tn} was not there., But the Constable when My L^d had Inform'd where the Cap$^{tn's}$ Lodgings were being there in Search of the Cap^{tn} did Seize this Inform^t and y^e Sword produced by the Constable is the Cap$^{tn's}$ Sword.

The Information of Dorothy the wife of Richard Browne of Howard Street taken upon Oath y^e 10th Day of Decemb. 1692

This Informant Sayth That Mrs Anne Bracegirdle Lodging in this Informants House came Home last night about 10 of Clock (much frighted) Her Mother and Mr Willm Page coming with Her., and She told this Inform^t Shee had been Sett upon by 6. Souldiers who would have forced Her into a Coach., and this Inform^t afterwards goeing into ye Street did there meett with the Ld Mohun and Cap^{tn} Hill with their Swords in their hands and this Inform^t asked them if they were the persons that had Soe rudely treated Mrs Bracegirdle as afores^d., And they told this Inform^t that they could have Carryed her away if they had been Soe aminded, for that they had a coach and Eight Pistolls charged therein., Whereupon this Inform^t call'd the Watch to Secure them and the Watch Endeavouring to Seize them the S^d Lord Mohun Said he was a Peer of the Realme and let ye watch touch Him if they Durst., and this Inform^t Saith that My L^d and the Cap^{tn} Staid there about an hour, and She heard ye Cap^{tn} Say he would be revenged before he went; And this Inform^t Saith that Some time after She Saw Mr Willm Mountford come into the Said Street and he went to My Lord and talked with Him and ye Cap^{tn} And My lord Said that he had a great deal of Respect and Hon^r for Him the Said Mountford., And presently after this Inform^t heard the S^d Cap^{tn} Hill Say to Mountford Draw to which Mountford answered he would and both their Swords were Drawne and they fought together, and Mountford Soon after went Homewards and the Cap^{tn} went away; And My Lord remained Still upon the place till the watch came and Secured Him.

The Information of Anne Jones Spinster taken upon Oath the Day and yeare aforesaid.

The Said Inform^t Saith That last night about Ten of ye clock Mrs Anne Bracegirdle came home crying with her Cloaths all Ruffled (her Mother Brother and Mr Page being in Company with her.) and this Inform^t Opened ye Door and Saw My Lord Mohun and Cap^{tn} Hill in the Street and She Shutt the Doore and afterwards this Inform^t went againe to Look out at the Door and then She Saw and Observ'd My L^d and the Cap^{tn} walking in the Street, and Soon after this Inform^t perceiv'd Mr Willm Mountford coming towards My lord and the Cap^{tn} from Norfolck Street, and when the Said Mounford came to them, She this Inform^t heard My Ld Say he had a Great Deal of Respect and Hon^r for Him the S^d Mountford and thereupon My Ld Embraced Him., and this Inform^t Saith that Soon after She Saw Cap^{tn} Hill come behind Mountford and gave Him a Box on the Ear and bid Him Draw., And this Inform^t presently after Saw both their Swords Drawne and then fighting., and this Inform^t heard Mountford's Sword break and Mountford thereupon went homeward and Cap^{tn} Hill the other way., And this Inform^t further Saith that My Ld Mohun had noe Sword Drawne During the Combat nor did he Stirr from the place till ye watch came & Secured Him.

The Information of Elizabeth walker Spinster taken upon Oath ye 10th day of Decemb. 1692

The S^d Inform^t Saith that She is Servt to Mrs Anne Bracegirdle and was last night after her Mistress came home, Sent to Mr Mountford's house to know if he was at home, and this Inform^t went to ye S^d Mr Mountford's House and from thence brought answer to her Mistress that the S^d Mountford was not at Home whereupon this Inform$^{t's}$ Mistress Sent her back againe to Mountford's House to Desire his wife to Send to Him and Desire Him to take care of Himself in Regard My lord Mohun and Cap^{tn} Hill who (She feared) had noe good Intention to Him did wait in the Street., and this Informant Saith that She and Mr Mountford's Maid went to Severall places to Enquire for ye Said Mr Mountford but did not find Him., And this Inform^t Saith that Shee did not See My Ld Mohun's Sword Drawne at any time as She passed to and fro by Him and Cap^{tn} Hill, but She Observed Cap^{tn} Hills Sword Drawne which She was told was occasioned by his loosing it's Scabbard, and this Inform^t Saith that about an hour after She had returned home from Enquiring after Mr Mountford the watch coming into the Street this Inform^t and Mrs Browne went to y^e Door and Soon after they Discovered Mr Mountford and Mrs Browne Endeavoured to hinder Him from coming into that Street and desiring him to goe home alledging My Ld Mohun and Cap^{tn} Hill were walking in the Street and the Cap$^{tn's}$ Sword was naked., But the S^d Mountford Notwithstanding the S^d Mrs Browne's Solicitation to the Contrary did goe to My Ld Mohun and mutuall Complim^{ts} past betweene them and this Inform^t heard Mountford Say he had a great Respect for My L^d and My lord answered that he had the like for Him and thereupon Embraced each other, And this Inform^t heard Mountford tell My L^d that it was a degrading to his Hon^r to keep Company with Such pittyfull fellow as Cap^{tn} Hill was or to the like Effect (and Cap^{tn} Hill was within hearing of these words) And My Ld Said to Mountford that the Cap^{tn} was a Man of Honnour, and this Inform^t Sayth that presently after She Saw the Said Mountford and the Cap^{tn} fighting with their Swords, And She heard Mountford Say He was kill'd and thereupon the Cap^{tn} fled in great hast and Mr Mountford went homeward and this Inform^t further Saith that the Ld Mohun Stood by in the Street all the time of the S^d fighting and did no way concern Himselfe therein as She observd and the watch Coming there presently after My L^d rendred Himself to the Same.

The Information of John Warrington taken upon Oath the 10th day of December 92

The S^d Inform^t Saith that last night about Ten or Eleven of Clock he did See from his owne doore two persons who (he is Since informed) were y^e Ld Mohun and Cap^{tn} Hill walking up and downe in the Street for about an hour and a halfe and this Inform^t Saith he Observ'd that y^e S^d Cap$^{tn's}$ Sword was drawne all the while and that My L^{ds} Sword was not drawne till the watch came and this Inform^t Saith that about a Quarter of an hour after, the watch had been gone out of the Street, this Inform^t Saw Mr Mountford goeing toward Mrs Browne's house, and Soon after Saw My Ld Mohun and Him the S^d Mountford Salute and Embrace each other., and presently after, this Inform^t Saw Cap^{tn} Hill and ye Said Mountford fighting with their Swords drawne, and this Inform^t heard that Mountford was wounded, and there being an outcry of Murder in the Street the watch came thither, And this Inform^t saith that he did not Observe ye Ld Mohun to have any hand in ye Quarrell, but Saith the S^d L^d did Stand by at the Corner of ye Street and went toward the watch, So Soon as it came into the Street, and further Saith not.

The Informa͠con of John Davenport and Willm Merry the Constable And Beadle of ye Dutchy Liberty taken upon Oath ye 10th xber 92

The Said Inform^{ts} Say that they being upon ye watch last night & goeing into Howard Street with ye S^d watch about Eleven of ye Clock did there find My Ld Mohun and Cap^{tn} Hill walking near Mrs Brace-girdle's Lodgings and this Inform^{ts} asking them what bussiness they had, they recd answer that one of them had a Sweet heart at ye next Doore and thereupon these Inform^{ts} left them there, and these Inform^{ts} further Saith that about an hour afterwards the S^d watch being then call'd for come into ye S^d Howard Street, these Inform^{ts} went thither againe with the watch & there found the Ld Mohun Standing with his Sword in his Hand in its Scabbard, and these Inform^{ts} hearing that there had been fighting Desir'd the S^d L^d to Deliver his Sword which He thereupon Deliver'd to the Inform^{ts} (the Constable) and alsoe renderd Himself to ye watch.

The Information of John Bancroft Surgeon taken upon Oath the 10th Decemb. 1692.

The S^d Inform^{ts} Saith that being Sent for He went about twelve of ye Clock last night to Mr Mountford's House and this Inform^t there found Mr Mountford very Desperately wounded on ye right Side of his Belly near the Short ribbe, And this Inform^t Saith that to the best of his Skill the S^d wound is mortall, this Inform^t having left ye s^d Mr Mountford this morning with an Intermitting and Languid pulse and in a cold faint and clammy Sweat and alsoe convulsive.

The Information of Ann Rudd widdow taken upon Oath ye Day and yeare as aforesd.

This Inform^t Saith that Cap^{tn} Richd Hill who Lodged in this Inform^{ts} House in Buckingham Court did yesterday morning Desire this Inform^t to lend Him a Suite of Night Linen and a Gowne and this Inform^t thereupon asking Him if he was goeing to Steale a Fortune the S^d Cap^{tn} answered noe., And this Inform^t after much Intreaty made by ye S^d Cap^{tn} did lend Him a Suite of Linen but not a Gowne and this Inform^t further Saith that She was Inform'd by her Servants that ye Ld Mohun had Lodged the two preceding Nights before the S^d Cap^{tn} borrow'd the S^d Night Linen as aforesd with ye S^d Cap^{tn} in this Inform^{ts} House and this Inform^t further Saith that ye S^d Cap^{tn} Hill came againe to his Lodgings yesterday in the afternoone and tooke thence Some Linen and a Night Gowne and he then asked this Inform^t to Lend Him a p̄re of Pockett pistols and this Inform^{ts} told him She had none neither did She know what they were.

The Examination of ye Right Honble charles Ld Mohun taken the Day and yeare aforesd.

The S^d Examinate Saith that he being last night in Company wth Cap^{tn} Hill did see Him ye s^d Cap^{tn} Hill and Mr Mountford fight together in Howard Street about Eleven of the Clock at night and ye S^d Examinate (after ye s^d fighting was ended) did see a peece of Mountfords Sword Lying upon the Ground there and ye watch Coming presently after into ye Street this Examinate rendring Himselfe to them and told them where ye Cap^{tn} Lodged.

The Information of Anne Bracegirdle Spinster taken upon Oath ye 10th of Decemb. 92

The S^d Inform^t Saith that She (together with her Mother and Brother) having Supt last night with Mr Page at his Lodgings in Princess Street near Covent Garden did come from thence about 10 of Clock and as they were going to ye Inform^{ts} Lodgings in Howard Street (this Inform^t being Led by Mr Page) a Souldier came and forced between this Inform^t and the s^d Mr Page and presently after 4 or 5. Souldiers more came and forcibly Endeavoured to put this Inform^t into a Coach (wherein was y^e

Ld Mohun) and this Inform^t thereupon cryed out & people coming to her Assistance the Souldiers Desisted (and this Inform^t Saith that Cap^tn Hill did then led this Inform^t Home and by ye way Expressed these words That he would have his revenge., And this Inform^t Saith that ye Cap^tn for a yeare last past has courted this Inform^t and that She had Denied his Suite, And this Inform^t further Saith that the Ld Mohun and Cap^tn Hill came yesterday morning to ye Play House (where this Inform^t is an Actress) and after ye rehearsall was over this Inform^t Observed the s^d Cap^tn to watch and Suspecting his Designe She hid Herselfe from Him but was discovered by ye s^d Ld Mohun and this Inform^t soon after made her Escape from them and afterward ye s^d Ld Mohun watched at One Door of ye Play House and Cap^tn Hill at ye other Door for Her this Inform^t for about an hour as this Inform^t was Informed, and then ye S^d L^d and Cap^tn went away together.

The Information of Gowen Page taken upon Oath ye Day and yeare afores^d.

The s^d Inform^t Saith that Mrs Bracegirdle her Mother and Brother Supt last night at his Lodgings in Princess Street and went from thence about 10 of Clock, and this Inform^t went to See them home and in their way Home a Souldier came and forced Himself betweene this Inform^t and Mrs Bracegirdle (whom this Inform^t was Leading.) and thereupon 4. or 5. Souldiers more did Endeauour forcibly to put Mrs Bracegirdle into a Coach in which was My Ld Mohun, And this Inform^t Seeing Cap^tn Hill with the Souldiers asked Him the meaning of it, And ye Cap^tn Having his Sword Drawne Struck at this Inform^t therewith, and this Inform^t Seeing the Blow to be aimed at his, this Inform^ts Head warded the Same off from his Head Soe that it fell upon his Hand and thereupon a great Company of People Coming about ye place ye S^d Souldiers by ye Ord^r of Cap^tn Hill did withdraw and kept of at Some Distance., And ye S^d Mrs Bracegirdle being much Disordred and seeing to be faint thereupon., the s^d Cap^tn Hill s^d He would Help Her Home to her Lodgings and Accordingly did lead Her thither, and this Inform^t went with them and when Cap^tn Hill had put Mrs Bracegirdle into her Lodgings this Inform^t stepping in after her was pulled by his Sleeve and Looking back the S^d Cap^tn Said he would Speak with Him a[nd] this Inform^t answered Him that to morrow would be time enough and this Inform^t Saith that about an hour after he (hearing an Out Cry of murder) went into ye Street and there Saw the Ld Mohun Deliver his

Sword to ye Constable and alsoe rendred Himselfe and this Inform^t went to Mr Mountford's House and found him Lying upon ye Floor in his owne parlour, And this Inform^t (after asking Him ye S^d Mountford how he d[id] and if he knew this Inform^t) asked Him if he Drew his Sword or made any Defense And ye s^d Mountford (answering ye S^d Questions) told this Inform^t that Cap^tn Hill run Him through before (he ye S^d Mountford) drew his Sword, And this Inform^t further Saith that the S^d Mountford is Since Dead of his S^d wound and farther Saith not

The Information of Mary the wife of ye aforesd Gowen Page taken upon Oath ye Day and yeare afores^d.

The S^d Inform^t Saith that her S^d Husband about 10. of Clock last night goeing with Mrs Bracegirdle to her Lodgings and Staying longer then this Inform^t thought necessary this Inform^t Sent her Servt to Enquire the Cause of his Stay and receiving an answere that his Stay was Occasioned by an attempt that was made to carry away Mrs Bracegirdle in a Coach this Inform^t thereupon went to Mrs Bracegirdle's Lodgings and Soon after this Inform^t att Mrs Bracegirdle's Desire went to Mr Mountford[s] House to Desire his wife to Send to her Husband and caution Him from coming home because My Ld Mohun and Cap^tn Hill were in the Street hard by waiting for Him and when this Inform^t was in Mr Mountford's House She hearing an outcry of Murder came to ye Door and Opened it, and there mett Mr Mountford coming in who laid his hand upon this Inform^t to Support Himselfe alledging that Cap^tn Hill had kill'd Him And ye Inform^t Help Him into his Parlour and this Inform^t Saith that as She passed in the Street between Mrs Bracegirdles Lodgings and Mr Mountford's House as afores^d She this Inform^t did See Cap^tn Hill and ye Ld Mohun in the Street with their Swords Drawne, and this Inform^t Saith that as Soon as She had helpt Mr Mountford into his Parlour as afores^d She went out and called for ye watch & told them Mr Mountford was kill'd, and this Inform^t Saw ye watch goe into Howard Street and My Ld Mohun was Standing there with his Sword in its Scabbard and this Informant coming near the S^d L^d He Desired this Inform^t to take Notice that he was not Concerned in Mr Mountford's Death., And ye S^d L^d thereupon Delivered his Sword to ye Constable and rendred Himselfe to ye watch and this Inform^t Saith that Mr Mountford's House is very neare Mrs Bracegirdle's Lodgings

The Information of Martha Bracegirdle widdow taken upon Oath ye Day and yeare afores^d.

The S^d Inform^t Saith That She and her Daughter Anne Bracegirdle and her Son Hamlet Bracegirdle having Supt last night at Mr Pages in Covent Garden and coming from thence about Ten of Clock and walking homewards were Stopt in Drury Lane by Severall Souldiers who Endeauoured to Thrust this Inform^ts Daughter into a Coach wherein ye Ld Mohun then was and this Inform^t Soon after Saw Cap^tn Hill Strike Willm Page and thereupon a Multitude of People flocking about them, the S^d Cap^tn Ordered ye Souldiers to Desist from Exeecuting their S^d Enterprise, and this Inform^t Saith that afterwards ye s^d Cap^tn accompanyed this Inform^t and her Company to their Lodgings in Howard Street and as they were goeing thither ye S^d Cap^tn told this Inform^t he would have revenge., and this Inform^t soon after they had arriv'd to ye S^d Lodgings She Saw ye Lord Mohun in the Street there with ye s^d Cap^tn and the S^d L^d thereupon told this Inform^t that She needed not to feare. for they had noe Dessigne but what was Honble and ye Inform^t further Saith that about 12. of Clock at Night which was an hour after the s^d L^d spoke with this Inform^t as afores^d She observd ye s^d L^d and Captn Hill walking up and Downe in the Street before ye Doore of her Lodgings and this Inform^t took notice that ye S^d Cap^tn's Sword was Drawne and that ye S^d Ld Mohun's Sword was not Drawne.

Ann Nevitt Lives in the house over against Mrs Bracegirdles Lodgeings, Says that when Capt Hill brought Mrs Bracegirdle home the doore was shutt against him, and that he desird of Mrs Bracegirdle Mother that he might see or speake with her daughter to aske her pardon that was refused and the Capt and my Lord Mohun walkt upon the flaggs before her Lodgeings and severall times as they walkt by knockt att the doore and desir'd they might either see or speake with Mrs Bracegirdle to aske her pardon and they would be gone and if it would not be granted they would walke there till they did see or speake with her, that psently she was makeing her Mistress bed and heard some stir in ye street and lookeing out of the window saw Hill pull his sword out of Mountfords body in the middle of the Street and run away that my Ld Mohun stood upon the flaggs wth his back against the wall his Sword in his hand butt not drawne, that my Lord perceiving what was done sayd he was not concerned and surrenderd himselfe up:

APPENDIX D

CAPTAIN RICHARD HILL

Information concerning Richard Hill is found in Charles Dalton, *English Army Lists and Commission Registers*, III, 270, IV, 297–298. The latter reference contains a reprint of a brief article which first appeared in *Notes and Queries*, 8th series, X, 1–2.

A statement of the case of Hill, published after Dalton's researches and not used by Forsythe, accompanies a petition addressed to Queen Anne (*MSS. of the Duke of Portland*, VIII, 321–322). It sets forth that Captain Richard Hill "was the son of the Dean of Kilkenny, and had colours given him at the age of thirteen in Lord Lisborne's regiment through the interest of his father-in-law, Captain Edward Carey, father of the present Lord Falkland. In a short time he was promoted to the command of a foot company in that regiment. At the end of the Irish war he left the company he then had in Brigadier Earle's regiment, and served two campaigns as a volunteer in Flanders, and returning to England had the misfortune at the age of sixteen to quarrel with Mr. Montford, and in a recontre to wound him, of which wound he died. This happened in 1692."

When one attempts to check these words with facts obtainable from other sources, one runs into many difficulties. In the first place, two statements cannot be reconciled: that Hill was the son of the dean of Kilkenny and that he was aged sixteen in 1692. Thomas Hill, B.A., Cambridge, 1655, M.A., 1659, D.D., 1670, was appointed prebendary of St. Patrick's Cathedral, Dublin, in 1667, and on March 11, 1671, he received the patent for the deanery of St. Canice, Kilkenny, to which he was admitted on March 18. He died on November 1, 1673, and was buried in the cathedral. In his will, dated March 3, 1672 [Is 167 2/3 intended?], he makes his wife Jane sole executrix and begs her to "be kind unto my poore deare children, Thomas, James, Richard, and that which she travels with. . . . Let her breed them up in the fear of God and they will prosper" (James Graves and John G. Augustus Prim, *The History, Architecture, and Antiquities of the Cathedral Church of St. Canice, Kilkenny* [Dublin, 1857], pp. 312–313). Thus Richard Hill must have been at least twenty years of age and possibly twenty-one or twenty-two in 1692. The present dean of Kilkenny, the Very Reverend Percy Phair, informs me that the extant baptismal records in St. Canice's Cathedral do not go back further than 1789. I am inclined to believe that Hill did not tell the truth about his age, feeling that the younger he appeared at the time of the killing, the more likely he would be to receive clemency. In 1704, the two persons who presumably had known his age when he had colors given him, Viscount Lisburne and Edward Carey, were dead.

Another troublesome statement is that Hill's father-in-law was Captain Edward Carey, father of Lord Falkland. Edward Carey (or Cary) of Caldicote (1656–1692) married Anne, daughter of Charles, Lord Lucas of Shenfield. They had two children — a son, Lucius Henry, born on August 27, 1687, who became the sixth Viscount Falkland upon the death of his second cousin, the fifth viscount, on May 24, 1694; and a daughter, Frances, who married in February, 1706, John Villiers, then Viscount Grandison, but later created earl (Vicary Gibbs, ed., *The Complete Peerage . . . by G. E. C.*, V, 242, VI, 77). If we are to take the word "father-in-law" in the generally accepted sense, we must assume that Edward Carey had a second daughter, whose existence has escaped the vigilance of genealogical researchers. If there was a second daughter, who married Hill, the wedding must have taken place after Carey's death in August, 1692. In December, Hill was thinking only of Anne Bracegirdle. If, on the other hand, we are to consider "father-in-law" in the sense of step-father, we must assume that

Edward Carey, before he married Anne, the daughter of Lord Lucas, had been the husband of the widowed Jane Hill. But there is no evidence of that fact, and it seems most unlikely.

Hill's first commanding officer, Viscount Lisburne, was appointed colonel, on March 8, 1689, of a regiment of foot that was raised principally in the county of Huntingdon (Dalton, III, 7). Schomberg wrote King William on December 30, 1689, concerning this regiment, which had been encamped at Dundalk: "My Lord Lisborne, dont le regiment est le plus foible, l'a fait passer fort. Il y a meslé 200 Irlandois. Je luy ay dit que l'intention de Votre Majesté n'etoit pas de meler des Irlandois parmy les regimens Anglois, mais de laisser des Irlandois aux regiments d'Iniskilling et Londonderry. La conduite du mylord Lisborne n'est pas bonne. Il passe la vie à jouer et boire. Peu de vin l'enyvre: apres cela, il tient des discours avec les officiers, qui vont jusque aux soldats, qui sont pernicieux au service. Puisque Votre Majesté lui a permis d'aller en Angleterre; je croy qu'il vaudroit mieux qu'il y demeura, et que son regiment fut mis dans un autre" (appendix to Sir John Dalrymple's *Memoirs of Great Britain and Ireland* [London, 1773], II, 11, 57). The regiment fought at the battle of the Boyne (July 1, 1690) and at Aghrim (July 12, 1691). On September 15, 1691, the commanding officer was killed before Limerick. The regiment remained encamped without the city until November 16, a month and a half after the articles of capitulation had been signed (George Story, *A Continuation of the Impartial History of the Wars of Ireland* [London, 1693], p. 285).

Since the fall of Limerick brought the Irish war to an end, and since Hill says that at the end of the war he had a company in Erle's regiment, he must have been under Erle's command before the date of his commission, March 21, 1692, when he, as captain in Lisburne's regiment, exchanged with Vincent Googene of Erle's regiment (Dalton, III, 270). Probably these commissions, made out at Whitehall, merely confirmed what had already taken place in Ireland. If Hill was with Erle in 1691, he would also have had an opportunity to see action at Aghrim. He was very likely in London during the early part of 1692, and it is not impossible that at this time he first became interested in the actress. In a deposition (see Appendix C), she alleged that the captain "for a yeare last past" had courted her. Later in the year, he was on the Continent, and with the other officers and men of Erle's regiment had a part in the disastrous day at Steenkirk. It is worth noting that Erle was present at the debate on the employing of foreign general officers held in the House of Commons on November 21, 1692. He there stated that at the engagement "the ground was mistaken, and so we were forced to retreat" (*The Parliamentary History of England*, ed. William Cobbett, V [1809], 718).

INDEX

INDEX